31 WAYS TO HAPPINESS

31 WAYS TO HAPPINESS

AWDHESH SINGH, PhD

One Of The Top Five Followed Writers Globally On Quora

wisdom tree

First published 2019

ISBN 978-81-8328-529-2

Published by
Wisdom Tree
4779/23, Ansari Road
Darya Ganj, New Delhi-110 002
Ph.: 011-23247966/67/68
wisdomtreebooks@gmail.com

Printed in India

Contents

Preface

We are the most blessed generation in the history of human race. Never before had there been so much material prosperity, freedom of thoughts and opportunities available to people. Even an ordinary person today can afford luxuries like car, air conditioners, televisions, computers and mobile phones, which were available only to the rich class just a generation ago. Middle class people are travelling around the world, eating out in good restaurants and spending huge amount of money for getting entertained.

However, despite all these material developments, the modern generation is perhaps the unhappiest generation of all time. They are suffering from poor health, obesity, stress at workplace and poor relationships with their friends and family. They are quite unhappy despite trying their best to be happy in their lives.

In order to be happy, we often follow the advices of our elders, life coaches, experts, psychologists and even spiritual gurus. We get many success formulae from them to achieve happiness. We follow them scrupulously to make our lives better.

We study hard in our childhood so that we can get good jobs and become happy. We work hard at our jobs so that we can earn more money, get faster promotions and thus become happy. We do everything possible to choose the right life partner and choose to marry the person whom we love, sometimes after long courtship and even live-in relationships so that our partner is compatible to us. Yet these relationships do not last long. We try our best to provide our children the best care and education, and yet the children leave us as they grow up and often find no time to spend with us.

Where are we going wrong?

Why are we not being able to fulfil our cherished desire to be happy?

Why getting everything else is easy, but happiness continues to be a mirage?

Some people believe that happiness is internal and comes from inside. They often leave all the worldly things and retire to a peaceful life only to realise that detachment does not give them happiness for long. They soon get bored of the life of solitude and come back to the worldly life to lead the same life again.

Some people try to achieve happiness through

external achievements. They earn huge wealth following by all of means. However, they soon find that wealth can only buy pleasure and comfort. They also discover that their senses need higher stimulation to achieve pleasure and it is impossible to satisfy the senses. They sometimes resort to intoxicants and drugs to get higher sensations and in the process damage their physical, mental and spiritual self forever.

31 Ways to Happiness explores the question of happiness at the deepest level. It does not provide any quick fix solution to make you happy. It tries to find the root cause of unhappiness and breaks our myths about happiness.

These 31 laws are not to be followed in any sequence and in many ways they are independent to each other. However, at the deeper level, we find that these laws are actually different organs of the same body or the branches of the same tree. They have no independent existence of their own.

These laws are eternal and discovered by the saints, philosophers and prophets in every era. Their value lies in their practical utility. I have myself been practising these laws in my life since years and found them as relevant and useful today as they were in the ancient times.

The real benefits of these laws flow to those who practice them. Just like you can't know the taste of a mango unless you taste one, you can't know the value of these laws unless you practice them in your life.

If you choose to practice these laws in your life in the right way, they can be the gateway of your happiness. When you are happy inside, you achieve success in whatever you do. Albert Schweitzer, a French-German theologian and philosopher said it aptly, 'Success is not the key to happiness. Happiness is the key to success. If you love what you are doing, you will be successful.'

We should not expect any overnight transformation in our lives just by knowing these laws. Practice and deeper understanding of these laws, however, can transform your long-held beliefs about happiness and change your life.

I am hopeful that the readers will find the *31 Ways to Happiness* a useful and valuable tool to make their life happier, healthier and successful.

—Dr Awdhesh Singh

1

Happiness is a Choice

Happiness is a choice. You can choose to be happy. There's going to be stress in life, but it's your choice whether you let it affect you or not.

—Valerie Bertinelli, American actor and television personality

We all desire happiness and wish to avoid suffering. Just like no one ever desires to be sick, similarly, no one ever desires to be unhappy. The famous Greek philosopher, Aristotle, once said, 'Happiness is the meaning and the purpose of life, the whole aim and end of human existence.'

John Lennon, an English singer and songwriter who co-founded *The Beatles*, shared, 'When I was five years old, my mother used to tell me that happiness was the key to life. When I went to school, they asked me what I wanted to be when I grew up. I wrote down "happy". They told me I didn't understand the assignment, and I told them they didn't understand life.'

Yet, an unfortunate reality is that most people are unhappy most of the time. Unhappiness is so widely pervasive in the modern world that if you tell someone that you are happy, people are unlikely to believe you. It is because we have stopped accepting that it is possible to achieve happiness. No surprise then that a leading psychiatrist, Thomas Szasz once said, 'Happiness is an imaginary condition, formerly attributed by the living to the dead, now usually attributed by adults to children, and by children to adults.'

Most adults believe that children are happier than them and, they have reasons for believing so. Unlike them, they say, children don't have the burden of supporting a family—financially and emotionally, they don't have to meet the never-ending deadlines and they don't have to please their bosses and clients. They don't have to run a household or take care of other family members. They can get what they want simply by demanding it from their parents.

Children, on the other hand, think that adults are happier. They want to grow up to be an adult and become independent as soon as possible. They are unhappy being children because neither do they have the freedom to do what they want nor the financial independence. They have to plead with their parents for everything. They have to get up, sleep and even play according to the will of their parents. Agreed, a child may not have to bother about paying the bills but we cannot ignore that she is always under pressure to attend classes, be disciplined at home and school, undergo assessments regularly and perform well in the seemingly never-ending examinations. Adults, on the other hand, have no schools, tests or any examinations to worry about.

> A child was being taken to school by her mother.
>
> The child saw, on the other side of road, a baby goat being taken forcefully by a horrible-looking man. The baby was crying profusely.
>
> The child asked the mother, 'Why is that baby crying so much?'
>
> The mother replied, 'Son! That man is taking it to a slaughterhouse for killing.'
>
> The child remarked, 'Oh! I thought that he is taking the baby to school.'

For most of the children, nothing is more torturous than going to school.

In short, the life of a child is no better than the life of adults from their point of view.

Happiness, therefore, appears to be an illusion and a distant goal for humanity.

However, there are still many who don't subscribe to this theory that it is impossible to be happy in this world. Some people believe that happiness is our natural state of being and we can be happy whenever we want to. Osho, a spiritual master, stated this belief boldly, 'Nothing is special in being happy—trees are happy, birds are happy, animals are happy, babies are happy. What is special in that? It is just the usual thing in existence. Existence is made of the stuff called happiness. Just look! Can't you see these trees...so happy? Can't you see the birds singing...so happily! Happiness has nothing special in it. Happiness is a very ordinary thing.'

How do we know that trees or birds are happy?

Do they even know what happiness is?

Man is unhappy because he knows what happiness is.

He is unhappy because he is unable to achieve this 'happiness', which, he thinks, other people have.

The Guilt of Happiness

Most people don't consider happiness as an important goal of life because happiness is an internal feeling and not an external achievement. Most people wish to achieve things that are discernible and acknowledged by the world as an achievement. They want success, power, fame, wealth—things that can be quantified as accomplishments. Happiness simply does not fit in the bill. Hence, many people don't consider happiness as an achievement.

We are living in a competitive world and have to perform better than others to achieve success. We also believe that it is success that brings happiness. We assume that if we can take care of success then success, itself, will take care of happiness. Therefore, people keep chasing success all through their lives as they consider happiness to be its by-product.

The only problem is that everyone can't be successful in every competition. For instance, if there are a thousand people participating in a race with only one trophy to be won, there will only be one winner and the rest will have to lose. As everyone except the one winner would have failed in the race, they would feel disappointed and unhappy because they had lined happiness with success.

Even the winner of the race can't remain happy for long because she would aim next to run with competitors of higher calibre and participate in national or international events. By this logic, only one person in the entire world can truly claim to be the world champion and will have the right to feel happy.

Unfortunately, even this world champion can't be truly happy since even if she wins in one race (say a 100-metre race), she can't win races of longer lengths or marathons. Even the top athlete of the world, in all categories, can't be happy because she still can't be the richest or most powerful person in the world. More so, her period of pinnacle in her own trade will be limited because another champion is bound to replace her in the future.

When we achieve success at any given point of time, we have a tendency to further the goalpost and therefore we keep chasing the illusion of happiness throughout our lives.

We are, thus, not chasing happiness but actually chasing unhappiness. We start feeling uneasy as soon as the initial euphoria or happiness from our achievement fades away. We then raise the bar further so that we can strive more and achieve even higher success thereby deliberately making ourselves unhappy. However, our lifelong chase of success only gives us suffering and unhappiness.

For many people it is almost a sin to be happy and content in this world because they believe that contentment hampers growth.

The Illusion of Happiness

If you believe that success is the route to happiness, it is highly unlikely that you can ever be happy for long. When you achieve success, you become happy for some time. However, such joy is temporary as, thereafter, you raise your aspirations and start seeking another achievement for happiness.

> There was a poor fisherman. Once, he was very hungry as he wasn't able to catch fish for many days. With great effort, he finally caught a big fish. He was extremely happy and planned to take the fish home to feed himself and his family. However, the fish started crying as soon as it was caught. It requested the fisherman to show mercy and spare its life. The fisherman was kind, and he put the fish back into the water.
>
> Suddenly the fisherman saw that the fish became a goddess. She told the fisherman, that she was a goddess who had become a fish due to a curse. The effect of the curse was

to be removed only if a kind man spared her life. So, she thanked the fisherman for his kindness and told him to ask her for a boon.

The fisherman was a simple man. He thought for a while and then he requested the goddess to give him a decent house, good clothes to wear and sufficient food to eat for a year.

The goddess granted him his wish immediately and promised that anytime he needed help, he may come to the same place near the sea and she will appear again to grant him another boon.

The fisherman on his return found that his hut was no longer there and that it had been replaced with a beautiful house. He found his wife and children dressed in expensive, wonderful clothes. The table, in the house, was laid with some of the best foods of the world. His happiness knew no bounds. He and his family enjoyed the comforts of life, blissfully, for many months.

Then, one day, when he was walking in the market, he was suddenly asked to move aside as the king of the state was passing down the same road. He was forcefully removed from the road by the king's guards. From a distance, he saw the king's caravan with the king himself seated on an elephant full of grandeur. He felt humiliated by the men of the king. Then he remembered the goddess and immediately went to the same place on the seashore and called out to her. The goddess appeared, as promised, and asked him to seek another boon. He requested that she must make him the king of the state. The boon was granted.

Now the man was incredibly happy. He had all the power and wealth of the state. He thought that finally all his desires were fulfilled and that he would lead a happy life forever.

One hot summer day, he was taking a tour of his state, sitting atop a gold-studded elephant. The weather was very hot and humid. He was sweating profusely. He looked at the sky and saw the sun shining like molten iron. He wished for some cool breeze but to no avail. He felt frustrated and went straight to the seashore and asked the goddess to appear.

The goddess asked, 'What do you need now?'

He said he wanted the sun to shine as per his orders and the wind to blow as per his wish.

The goddess got terribly angry and said contemptuously, 'You fisherman! I made you a king. Still, you are not satisfied. Go and become a fisherman again.'

This is how the nature of man is. He is always craving for more and more. His desires are so high that even God can't satisfy them.

The Choice of Happiness

While it is impossible to be happy if we link happiness to achievements and success, it is possible to be happy right now, if you choose to be.

An American investment banker was at the pier of a small coastal Mexican village when a modest boat with just one fisherman docked. In the boat were several large Yellowfin tuna fish. The American complimented the Mexican on the quality of his fish and asked him how long it took him to catch them.

The Mexican replied, 'Only a little while.'

The American then asked the fisherman why he didn't stay out longer to catch more fish.

The Mexican said that since he had enough to support his family's immediate requirements he did not feel the need for it.

The American then asked, 'But what do you do with the rest of your time?'

The Mexican fisherman said, 'I sleep till late, fish a little, play with my children, take siestas with my wife, stroll the village each evening where I sip wine, and play guitar with my amigos. I have a full and a busy life.'

The American scoffed, 'I am a Harvard MBA and can help you. You should spend more time fishing and with the proceeds from extra fish, buy yourself a bigger boat. With a bigger boat, you can catch even more fish and from the money you earn, you can buy several boats. Eventually you will have a fleet of fishing boats. Then, instead of selling your catch to a middleman you can sell directly to the processor and someday open your own cannery too. You will be able to control the product, processing and distribution. In the course of time, you can leave this small coastal fishing village and move to Mexico City, and then to Los Angeles and thereafter to New York City, where you can run your expanding enterprise.'

The Mexican fisherman asked, 'But, how long will all this take?'

To which the American replied, '15-20 years.'

'But what then?' asked the Mexican.

> The American laughed and said, 'That's the best part. When the time is right you can announce an IPO and sell your company's stocks to the public and become very rich. You will make millions!'
>
> 'Millions! Then what?' asked the fisherman.
>
> The American said, 'Then you can retire. Move to a small coastal fishing village where you can sleep till late, fish a little, play with your kids, take siestas with your wife, stroll to the village in the evenings where you can sip wine and play your guitar with your amigos.'
>
> 'But, that is what I am doing now. Why take such a long path?' said the smiling fisherman.

Who can destroy the happiness of this poor man, who is happy even in his so-called poverty?

If you desire, you can choose to be happy here and now. If you don't choose happiness, you will possibly remain unhappy even after becoming the richest, the most powerful and the most famous person of the world. William Shakespeare rightly said, 'There is nothing either good or bad, but thinking makes it so.'

If you wish to be happy, you have to choose happiness over wealth, power, success or fame. You have to accord happiness the highest priority in life.

2

Happiness is a Stream of Experiences

Experience is not what happens to a man. It is what a man does with what happens to him.

—Aldous Leonard Huxley,
English writer and philosopher

Swami Parthasarathy, an Indian philosopher, has described life as a 'series of experiences' also known in Sanskrit as *Anubhav Dhara*. He adds, 'Experiences flowing one after another is life. When the flow stops, life is extinct. An experience, therefore, is a unit of life, just as a brick is a unit of a building. They, in effect, constitute your life. If they are happy, you are happy. If they are unhappy, you are unhappy. As your experiences, so is your life…and the stream of experiences is life.'

Happiness, therefore, has two components:

1. Individual (the subject)
2. The world (the object)

Hence, if we wish to lead a happy life, we must have more happy experiences in our life. Gathering these happy experiences requires not only improving ourselves, but also improving the world around us.

When you are seriously sick, very little can make you happy even if you are living in an air-conditioned house with the best of food, and all luxuries of life at your disposal. Similarly, if there is no food, no water, no house and the temperature is soaring to 55 degrees centigrade, even if you are perfectly healthy, you won't be happy.

In order to be happy, we must have a harmonious relationship with the external world.

We are the World

We and our world are not different just as a drop of a sea and the sea are not different. We are the world and the world is us. Just like every single cell in the body of a person has the same DNA, we too are a microcosm of everything that is out there in the world. We have evolved with the world and we are one with it. Ancient saints in India had coined a beautiful term—*Aham Brahmasmi*—that means 'I am the world', or in a more expansive term 'I am the universe'. The Upanishads also stated the same fact more than two thousand years ago.

> *As is the human body, so is the cosmic body.*
> *As is the human mind, so is the cosmic mind.*

As is the microcosm, so is the macrocosm.
As is the atom, so is the universe.

We have the mind and the consciousness of the universe. Due to our ignorance, we see the world and our own selves divided and separated into two units. A truly wise person sees the entire world in the self and the self in the world. Lord Krishna expounded: 'The man equipped with "yoga" looks at all with an impartial eye, seeing self in all beings and all beings in self. He who sees Me everywhere and everything in Me, is never separated from Me nor I from him.' (*Gita 6:29-30*)

When we see the world superficially, we see individuals who appear independent of each other. We fail to see through our senses how deeply connected we are with each other at the spiritual level.

Take an example of an inanimate object like your bed. It is made of wood that at some point of time was a tree, nourished by air and water from the Earth and by sunlight. Then a man cut the tree, and the wood was sent to a factory to be converted into timber. The timber was purchased by a carpenter who designed and made the bed using several tools made of iron, that were manufactured in some factory in some part of the world. The timber was polished by various chemicals and sent to the shop for sale. The shop was made up of concrete and bricks with the help of a large number of people and used electricity, bulbs, fans and many more things that were produced by some power company which employs thousands of people.

If you use your imagination, you can easily find a connection to everyone and everything and discover the contribution of almost everyone in your life.

Interdependence of Humanity

Human lives are so deeply interconnected with each other that we can't live in this world as an independent person of our own. Everyone in the world is an extension of the self. When others are suffering, we too can't escape suffering. Our happiness depends on others and their happiness depends on us. William Blake, the English poet, has defined it beautifully:

To see a world in a grain of sand
And heaven in a wild flower,
Hold infinity in the palm of your hand
And eternity in an hour.

We are like a miniature world and our mind is like a miniature mind of the world. Even when we isolate ourselves from the world completely, by going to an isolated place, our mind does not get completely detached from the world. It is constantly moving in the past and future and interacting with many people, in our imagination.

- Sometimes, we are having a conversation with our children, parents, spouse, boss or friends.
- Sometimes, we are upset because someone shouted at us and we could not reply back.
- Sometimes, we are feeling guilty as we have shouted at someone unnecessarily.

- Sometimes, we are making plans for our future.
- Sometimes, we are worried about our adversaries.
- Sometimes, we are rejoicing about our achievements from the past.
- Sometimes, we are feeling guilty about having done something wrong in the past.

While there is a limitation of time and space in the physical world, there is none in our imagination. We can go back thousands of years or imagine things and events hundreds of years ahead. We can communicate with a person dwelling in any other part of the world through our imagination. We can even communicate to scientifically non-existent entities like ghosts, devils and gods through our imagination.

Hence, the stream of experiences of life includes not only our actual experiences with the world but also our imaginary experiences in the mind. And, the emotions created through our imagination are no different from the emotions created in our real-life interactions. We sometimes make our lives miserable owing to the imaginary experiences of our own making. Michel de Montaigne, one of the most significant philosophers of the French Renaissance, has aptly said, 'My life has been full of terrible misfortunes most of which never happened.'

Harmonising Within

We know there is a lot of conflict in the world. We know it because our newspapers and news channels are full of reports on it. There is crime against individuals as well as criminal activities against nations such as terrorism and organised corporate frauds. People are almost always engaged in a fight with each other for their survival and growth.

Now, imagine a situation where you don't have access to any visual or print media. You would hence be unaware of what is going on in the rest of the world. However, shutting your eyes and ears to the happenings of the outside world does not make the world more peaceful. People would still be killed by terrorists, maybe thousands of miles away from your home, in some part of the world; thousands of people would still die in road accidents—crimes would still happen in the world as usual.

While it may not be a good idea to take excessive interest in the happenings of the world, it is also not desirable to shut your eyes to it and become aloof and indifferent to the pains or joys of others. It is our awareness of the world that provides us an opportunity to learn from the experience of others—a bad experience that someone has gone through prompts us to take precautions and protect ourselves from a similar fate. Otto von Bismarck, a statesman from the erstwhile country of Prussia, remarked, 'Only a fool learns from his own mistakes. The wise man learns from the mistakes of others.'

Just like the conflicts that happen in the outside world, conflicts also occur within our inside worlds—our minds. The reasons for the conflicts in the inside world are almost the same as that of the outside world—they are because of conflicting desires but this time within ourselves.

- We desire to be honest but we also want to get lots of wealth even if it requires using unfair means.
- We desire to be moral but we also want to have immoral pleasures.
- We desire to maintain or lose weight but we also want to enjoy fatty fast foods or other high-calorie delicacies.
- We desire to become more knowledgeable but our mind is unable to concentrate and distracts us from sitting down to read.

What is good for the body is often rejected by the senses. For example, simple food such as fruits, green vegetables and/or freshly-cooked home food are good for our body but may not be liked by our senses. Our senses make up for the source of our pleasures and they usually seek exotic, tasty and high-calorie food. Our mind knows that such food is bad for health, but irrespective of that, the senses desire such food. However, the pleasure of relishing such food is only momentary. Once you finish eating these delicacies, you realise how many extra calories you may have consumed or how the excess oil and flavour-enhancers will affect your digestion, and almost immediately you start feeling guilty.

You can observe the numerous conflicts going on inside your mind all the time. The more intense the conflict, the more you suffer.

When we are fully integrated within, all our internal conflicts melt away just like a hypothetical society where there is negligible conflict because people are emotionally attached to each other.

Transforming Our Life Experiences

Once we understand that our happiness is the result of our life experiences with the world, we will also understand the importance of taking care of both our external and internal world. We can't be happy if our children are unhappy, our spouse is unfaithful or if our boss hates us. It is futile to focus just on internal changes and hope to attain long-lasting happiness.

> There was a woman who used to come to a meditation class. She practised all the exercises and meditation techniques in the class faithfully.
>
> Her instructor, however, noticed that she was still quite irritated and unhappy. One day she asked the lady the purpose of her joining the meditation class.
>
> The lady said, 'I am quite disturbed because I have a big loan to pay off. I decided to join the class so that I can get some peace of mind with meditation.'
>
> The instructor listened to her story and then advised, 'Meditation can't give you the peace of mind you are looking for. You should rather spend two extra hours at your work place and earn extra money so that you can repay the loan quickly. This would be a more effective treatment for your tortured mind than any form of meditation.'

You have to fix the problems in the external world to enjoy lasting happiness. You must manage the people of your world—your children, your family, your colleagues, your friends and relatives well to have happy experiences with them. But, the good news is that your world is much smaller than the world that consists of billions of people. Ninety per cent of your experiences pertain to the people of your little world—your friends, family, neighbours and your colleagues. They are hardly a few dozen people. If your experiences with them are good, the rest of the world would not be able to disturb your happiness much.

3

Happiness is Subjective

It is pretty hard to tell what does bring happiness; poverty and wealth have both failed.

—Kin Hubbard, American cartoonist and journalist

One day Buddha was sitting in a forest with some monks. Everyone had an excellent lunch and was enjoying each other's company. A farmer, who looked very unhappy, passed by. He asked the Buddha and the monks if they had seen his cows somewhere. Buddha replied in negative.

The farmer said, 'Monks, I'm so unhappy. I had twelve cows and I don't know why but they have all run away. I also have a few acres of a sesame seed plantation but the insects have eaten up everything. I am suffering so much that I think I am going to kill myself.'

Buddha said, 'My friend, we have not seen any cows passing by here. You might want to look for them in the other direction.'

The farmer thanked him and ran away. Buddha turned to his monks and said, 'My dear friends, you are the happiest people in the world. You don't have any cows to lose. If you had as many cows to take care of, you would have been very busy.' He continued, 'That is why, in order to be happy, you have to learn the art of releasing the cows. You release the cows one by one. In the beginning you thought that those cows were essential for your happiness and you got more and more cows. But now you realise that cows are not really conditions for your happiness; they are, in fact, an obstacle to your happiness. That is why you must release your cows.'

The above wisdom coming from Gautam Buddha holds water because he not only preached releasing the cows but practised it as well. He left all his wealth and power as the prince of Kapilvastu to discover the truth about life.

Only a person who has had the experience of being rich as well as poor can say what circumstance is superior—being rich or being poor. Most people are either rich or are poor and know only one side of the story. The rich people are unlikely to release their cows because they believe that acquiring cows is the source of happiness. In the same way, the poor man hardly knows the joys of the rich man since he himself never had much wealth.

Happiness is thus a subjective thing.

Most people don't have an experience of both sides of the reality and hence they can't really decide, objectively, which one is better. If they are happy with their present, they are likely to believe that their present state is the source of happiness and therefore must be better than other alternatives. It is like being happy with your spouse or children. You tend to believe that your spouse is the best and your children are the best. Such an experience is purely subjective as it is not possible to measure or evaluate your experience with other alternatives.

However, if some people are unhappy with their present state, they are likely to think that everyone else is better than them and that their present circumstances are responsible for all their sufferings. As most people are unhappy in the world, they find the grass to be greener on the other side of the fence, without knowing that possibly the person on the other side of the fence is looking at them, and the grass on their side, with the same feelings.

Knowledge Transforms People

If you are a teetotaller, you may not know the joy of drinking alcohol. Similarly, a drinker may not know the bliss of being a teetotaller. Our experience changes our perception of happiness.

Daniel Gilbert, American psychologist and writer, explains in his book *Stumbling on Happiness*:

> Our experiences instantly become part of the lens through which we view our entire past, present and future, and like any lens, they shape and distort what we see.
>
> Once we learn to read, we can never again see letters as mere inky squiggles. Once we learn about free jazz, we can never again hear Ornette Coleman's saxophone as a source of noise. Once we learn that Van Gogh was a mental patient,

or that Ezra Pound was an anti-Semite, we can never again view their art in the same way.

You can't become an illiterate person again once you have become literate.

You can't think like a teetotaller once you have become alcoholic.

Every piece of knowledge and every experience of your life transforms you forever and you are never the same person again.

Let me elucidate the subjectivity of perception with an example.

There are thousands of languages spoken all around the world (an estimated 6909) and we can, at best, understand only a few. Let us say that you can't read or speak Tamil, a language popular in South India. Now if you were to see a signboard in Tamil or a person spoke to you in Tamil, it would make no sense to you. You won't know if what he spoke to you were sacred words of a scripture, a political propaganda or an abuse. However, once you learn the language and understand it, the same words start making sense to you. Thereafter, it would be impossible for you not to understand these words and get influenced by the message contained in these words.

You can't be ignorant after you have acquired a piece of knowledge or you have undergone an experience in life.

The famous American philosopher, Ralph Waldo Emerson wisely said, 'The mind, once stretched by a new idea, never returns to its original dimensions.'

You See the World As You are

You become what you know and what you do.

You see the world not as it is but as you are.

Our concept of happiness is always subjective. It is based on our perception of things that comes from our life's experiences. As no two individuals ever get an identical series of experiences, the perspective will be unique and different for everyone.

I am a teetotaller, non-smoker and a vegetarian. However, I have many friends who are regular drinkers, smoke and love their non-vegetarian preparations. I can't understand why they do so in spite of knowing the many ill-effects of smoking and drinking. I feel happy that I am not one of them. However, my friends, who drink and smoke, can't have fun in their lives without drinking and smoking. No party is complete for them if there are no drink or meat delicacies on the menu.

While I think I am happier and better than them, how can I be sure if what I think is right? Is it not possible that I am missing the joy of drinking, smoking or eating meat?

In order to really compare the two, I must actually become a drinker, smoker and a non-vegetarian. As I am unlikely to do this, my understanding of happiness is going to be biased.

As we won't let go off our habits easily, we may continue to believe in the happiness of what we are doing or how we are existing unless something drastically changes in our way of living which forces us to change our perception.

Even if we change our habits and decide to live both sides of the life, we still can't fully assess the relative merit of each experience. The perception of a poor-turned-wealthy person and a wealthy-turned-poor person can't be the same even though both of them have undergone the experience of being rich as well as poor.

How do we then decide who is happy and who is not?

Every person who is satisfied, content and happy thinks his understanding of happiness is truest because that is what he is experiencing. So, a virtuous person would subscribe his happiness to his virtuous deeds while an evil person would subscribe his happiness to his vices. Since a corrupt person has never lived a virtuous life, he will possibly never know the euphoria one derives from doing good deeds.

Just like a sinner can't know the joys of living an honourable life, a virtuous person can't know the joys of a sinful life either.

A government officer, if corrupt, can make much more money in a single deal, through illegal bribes, than what an honest government officer would make from his salary over several years. A corrupt man enjoys all luxuries of life and possesses the ability to engage the best of the advocates to defend himself before the courts, if he is ever caught.

When an honest man finds a corrupt officer being arrested and prosecuted, he feels happy and his belief in following the righteous path gets strengthened.

One of our family friend's son committed suicide a

few years ago. The father was an upright officer, living a very modest life. When I met his family in their home after the incident, his wife was inconsolable. She squarely blamed the honesty of her husband for the death of her child. The son used to write a diary regularly and he had expressed his anguish over the inability of his father to finance his admission in a private engineering college, while all his friends had gained admission in the same college with their parents' ill-earned money or so he assumed. His father told me, in confidence that he had always thought that being honest was the best way of living. However, after the loss of his child, he developed serious doubts about the virtues of honesty.

When a virtuous person suffers in his life, he ascribes his sorrow to his virtues. In the same way, when an unethical person suffers due to his vices, he blames his vices for the problems. You can't really know if it is better to be virtuous or vile. You would perhaps decide it on the basis of your own temperament and whether you are happy with your present set of circumstances or not.

We can't claim others to be unhappy if they are following a different path from us just because we are happy walking down our chosen path. We also can't claim others to be happy if they are following a different path from us, because we are unhappy with our path.

4

Repair Your Past

Study the past, if you would divine the future.

—Confucius

There is a very popular science-fiction movie *Back to the Future,* produced by Steven Spielberg. In this 1980s classic, the main protagonist, a teenager named Marty McFly, gets accidentally thrown back to the year 1955 where he meets his future parents when they were still in high school. Marty has a crisis when he attracts his young mother's attention but he fixes this damage to history and makes his parents-to-be to fall in love so that his existence is not in danger and then returns to the present. The movie was the most successful film of the year, grossing more than $383 million worldwide and receiving widespread critical acclaim. It also won several awards.

The reason for the success was that it echoed our secret desire: a whimsical wish to be able to go back in the past and rectify our mistakes so that we can have a better present and a brighter future. Unfortunately, it is impossible to go back in the past as in order to do that we have to travel faster than light which is inconceivable as of now, though shown frequently in movies and novels. Logically, it has been explained that it is unreasonable to go back in the past, because if it was possible, one could go back and maybe accidentally interfere in one's parents coming together or kill them before one was born. In such a situation, one won't exist; but that is impossible since he does exist! Hence, rationalists have concluded that going back in the past is impossible.

This argument may hold good for the physical body, but we know that our mind can easily travel, not just in the past, but also in the future. In fact, most of us spend a lot of our time dwelling in our past and future and often fail to live in our present. Several thousand years ago, Buddha advised, 'Do not dwell in the past, do not dream of the future, concentrate the mind on the present moment.'

The question that arises is, 'Why does our mind not live in the present?'

Our mind is free from the limitation of time and space. We can think about a life in America while being physically present in India. We can also think of past events that happened several years ago and actually live the joy or the pain of that moment again simply through our past experience.

Happiness is a state of mind, so our miseries and

joy come from living in any of the three dimensions of time—past, present and future. Hence, if we wish to live happily, we must learn to remove sufferings not only from the present, but also from the past and future. This can be done by understanding how our mind works.

Functioning of the Mind

Imagine you are visiting one of the most exotic locations of the world. This is the place that you have always dreamt about going to. You worked hard, accumulated money and now you are present in the place of your dreams. You see beautiful mountains and unparalleled scenic beauty. Everywhere you look, you find nature in its purest and most pristine form. You are feeling overwhelmed with all the beauty around you.

Now imagine that somehow the previous night, you had developed a severe toothache. The pain is excruciating. Now, will you still be able to enjoy the beauty of nature?

The answer is 'no'.

Our one pain has the power to distract us from all the pleasures of the world. We can be happy in the present only when we are free from all the pains and sufferings of the past and a probable future.

Suppose I advise you to concentrate only on nature and forget about the pain. Can you do it? If you are like most people, it would be nearly impossible for you to ignore pain and enjoy the present. The only solution would be to take some powerful drug or medicine that will curb the pain momentarily and will let you enjoy the beauty around you.

Think of your mind as a timeless entity that is spread across the past, the present and the future—from infinite to infinite. It has no beginning and no end. Hence, if there is any pain in any frame of your mind—in past, present or in an imagined future—you will suffer it and fail to enjoy the present moments. No way will you be able to enjoy happiness in the present, unless you reduce and, preferably, eliminate all pain from your mind.

This consciousness of past–present–future is eternal and is often referred to as soul.

Our mind is working all the time with two goals in sight: first is to minimise the pain and the second is to maximise the happiness. In its attempt to achieve its twin objectives, it is always moving back and forth in the three dimensions of time so that it can heal the pain and bring happiness to the present.

Living in the Past

We spend quite a lot of time everyday thinking about our past. The more experience you have in your life, the more past you must have accumulated. It makes sense to think that older people live more in the past than the younger generation, which spends more time dreaming about their future.

At this moment, when you are reading this book, your mind may not be in the present. It is possible you may have remembered something from your past or are thinking about the future.

When we are doing something that is giving us

pleasure, we remain in the present and don't think about the past. However, if the act is not pleasant (for example, if you are not enjoying what you are reading or are sitting in a boring lecture in the classroom), your mind would travel either to the past or to the future.

You may perhaps remember how your boss humiliated you before your subordinates a few days ago and you could not retaliate. Or, you may be worried about the examination that is going to take place after a few days for which you are not adequately prepared. Similarly, you may start dreaming of the good time that you can have in the near future once the boring class is over. In that present moment, since your mind is focused on these thoughts, you start experiencing the pain or the pleasure as if it was happening just now. Once the feeling of pain or pleasure of the past or future takes over, you just can't concentrate on the present anymore.

You may feel upset for not being in the present or not being able to enjoy a book or have an interesting conversation with your spouse or friends, but you simply can't live in the present if your mind is suffering from any form of pain from the past or imagined pain from the future. While you can take care of your present physical pain by taking medicines, there is no quick-fix solution to take away the pain of the past and future from your mind. People often resort to alcohol or drugs to intoxicate the mind so that it can get distracted, however momentarily, from the emotional pain that is bothering them.

If you don't fix the problems of your past and future, you may lose the joy of the present. You may become susceptible to falling for alcohol, drugs or other forms of intoxicants to calm your mind and to be able to live in the present.

Addiction

One way, used by many people, to get rid of painful thought is to take alcohol or drugs that can lift the mood and numb the negative emotions, albeit, for some time. But as soon as one is sober, the painful thoughts are back again. Eckhart Tolle, the author of *The Power of Now: A Guide to Spiritual Enlightenment*, wrote, 'Every addiction arises from an unconscious refusal to face and move through your own pain. Every addiction starts with pain and ends with pain. Whatever the substance you are addicted to—alcohol, food, legal or illegal drugs, or a person—you are using something or somebody to cover up your pain.'

He concludes, 'If it weren't for alcohol, tranquillisers, antidepressants, as well as the illegal drugs, which are all consumed in vast quantities, the insanity of the human mind would become even more glaringly obvious than it is already.'

If we really wish to enjoy lasting happiness in our life, our conscience must be cleaned off all the pains of past, present and future.

Clearing Your Conscience

Imagine you are a happily married man who has a beautiful wife and two children. You are highly respected in the society and known to be upright, honest and principled. You meet an extremely charming woman and fall in love with her. You clandestinely meet her. One night you go to a hotel, under a false name, and make love to her. After a couple of days, you learn it from the newspapers that the owner of the same hotel is arrested by police for making secret videos through hidden cameras planted in the hotel rooms. The police claim to have seized several explicit video clips from the possession of the owner of the hotel.

You will now be a deeply worried man because of the consequences occurring from the eventuality of the police coming across a video of you and your lover. The police may call you for an interrogation. You feel even more scared of the thought of your video having been already uploaded on some online pornographic site. You feel devastated. The more you think about it, the more you worry. Your mind is fully occupied in finding out ways and means to overcome this problem and avoid the pain which you may face in future if the video is made public or if it becomes known that you are also one of the victims. Your past haunts you all the time. Your conscience gets filled with great pain whenever this incident comes to your mind.

Sometimes even smaller issues can become a source of pain for you. Imagine in a party, you passed some nasty comments about your boss. Now you are worried because many of your colleagues were also present in the party, including a few who were quite close to your boss. You start visualising the prospect of them telling your boss about your nasty comments and the boss retaliating in an unpleasant manner.

Paradoxically, the tendency of your mind to travel across the three dimensions of time is not only a source of pain but also of pleasure. Just like you get depressed and start worrying as soon as your mind catches your evil deeds, it also makes you happy when it relives the great moments of your life. Imagine yourself saving the honour of a woman by risking your life and the society decorating you with accolades. Even several years later, every time you remember those moments, or someone mentions your name in regard with that great act of bravery, you suddenly feel overcome with a surge of happiness.

Your conscience is not only the repository of your failures but also of your successes. It contains your vileness as also your goodness. The more good deeds you have performed in the past, the more happiness will be at your disposal all the time. You can always borrow some of that happiness when you are feeling low.

When your mind is dwelling on a past event, it is not for giving you pain in the present, but it is actually reminding you of an unsolved matter or an uncared wound that needs to be attended to, to get relief from the pain. Instead of ignoring that pain, it would be better if you accept it and find a way to reduce it by taking a suitable action.

One way to take care of an unpleasant past is to learn the lessons from your past mistakes and not repeat them. If you can learn that being unfaithful is a source of lasting pain, though it may give you joy temporarily, and take a vow not to be adulterous in future, you may soon stop thinking of the past as bitter since it has helped you lead a better life.

In the same way, if you can learn the lesson that virtuous deeds are like happiness deposits in your life, and can always be used to bring you comfort in your low moments, you would do more and more virtuous deeds and make your life better.

When your mind is free from pains of the past, you start making a beautiful future for yourself by doing the right deeds in the present.

Your good deeds of today become the source of your happiness for tomorrow. You thus start becoming positive in life and your mood changes. Thus, your life is filled with happiness from the lovely memories of the past, hope for the future and joy in the present.

5

The Source of Joy and Sorrow are the Same

The greatest happiness is to know the source of unhappiness.
—Fyodor Dostoyevsky, Russian novelist and philosopher

We know the distinction between good and bad food, good and bad habits and good and bad actions. We know that certain things such as cigarettes and illicit drugs are harmful for health. We know that fatty, spicy and high-calorie food can damage our health. We also know that fruits, salads and vegetables are beneficial for health. We are aware that we must exercise regularly to stay in good shape and be fit. It is, therefore, possible for a disciplined and a knowledgeable person to avoid what is improper and follow what is correct to maintain a healthy life.

Similarly, how good would it be, if we could identify what gives us happiness and what gives us pain. We would have to follow the habits that give us happiness—such as following the principles of integrity, honesty, love, compassion and so on—and avoid everything that gives us pain. But, in reality, we fail to achieve happiness even after doing all this as the source of happiness and pain is the same. What gives us the greatest joy is also the source of our greatest pain. Let us understand this mystery of life.

Love

What is life without love? Mahatma Gandhi said, 'Where there is love, there is life.' Love is even compared to godliness. Some saints have also expounded that love is the source of ultimate knowledge and wisdom. We all know that a loveless life is not worth living. We all want to love and be loved. Yet it is also a fact that love can be the greatest source of pain for many people.

It is said that when we love, our souls become one with our beloved. However, the unification of souls often becomes a great source of pain because we tend to suffer every time our beloved suffers. You thus multiply your pain when you fall in love.

It may be blissful when in love but your suffering also multiplies at the same time.

Family

'Family is not an important thing,' said Michael J Fox, 'it's everything'. Who doesn't know the importance of a family? We could not have survived in this world but for the love and support of our parents and family members.

A family is a small world created by us that is bound together with love. We believe that our family loves us unconditionally and feel at home with them. We love our family and treat it as the greatest gift of God.

Yet, family often becomes a source of pain when there is disharmony and acrimony amongst the family members. Living with the same family then becomes hell instead of heaven, especially when love and trust is lost. The following story explains both sides of a family.

> It seems that Reagan and Gorbachev arranged a competition to determine whose nation had the bravest troops. The two leaders arrived, at the designated hour, on a plateau in Finland high above the water. Each was accompanied by a battalion of crack troops, smartly uniformed. The leaders shook hands.
>
> Reagan went first. He addressed his battalion of Marines.
>
> 'Private Jones! Front and centre.'
>
> Private Jones saluted and briskly marched to the front of the ranks, facing his commander.
>
> 'Private Jones! March to the edge of the cliff.'
>
> Private Jones saluted and briskly marched to the very edge of the cliff.
>
> 'Private Jones! Jump!'
>
> Jones just stood there, unmoving.
>
> 'Private Jones! I said jump!'
>
> The man's knees started to shake, but he was otherwise motionless.

'Private Jones! This is your Commander-in-Chief. I order you to jump.'

Private Jones wailed out, 'I can't! I have a wife and a family!'

The American soldiers arrived and escorted Jones away for court martial. Reagan backed off in disgrace. It was now Gorbachev's turn.

'Comrade Dmitrivich! Front and centre.'

Comrade Dmitrivich saluted and briskly marched to the front of the ranks, facing his commander.

'Comrade Dmitrivich! March to the edge of the cliff.'

Dmitrivich saluted and briskly marched to the very edge of the cliff.

'Comrade Dmitrivich! Jump!'

Dmitrivich jumped off the cliff.

By some miracle, he gets snagged on a branch and lands on a crag some 50 feet below the top of the cliff. Dmitrivich is badly injured, but still alive and conscious. He is carried away on a stretcher.

As Dmitrivich is carried past Private Jones, Jones cannot resist asking him,

'Dmitrivich! How could you do it? How could you jump?'

Dmitrivich answered, 'I had to! I have a wife and a family.'

Wealth

Most of us believe that wealth is the greatest source of happiness. People sacrifice everything to earn wealth with the hope that it will lead to happiness. Undoubtedly, wealth can provide us with worldly pleasures, comforts, status in the society and even fame, but it is noteworthy that our greatest source of pain is also wealth.

The life of wealthy people is riddled with challenges and insecurities. There are many who are coveting their wealth. They may be surrounded by selfish people who are only interested in their money and not in the person they are. The threat to their life increases when they are wealthy. They are always in stress attempting to preserve this wealth as they are scared of losing the wealth to theft, frauds and bad investment decisions. Also, erroneous purchase decisions, as an offshoot of this wealth, can lead to illegal, unhealthy or immortal activities.

People chasing wealth have to work harder, take more risks and even perform some illegal and immoral acts to acquire greater wealth.

Wealth can also misguide one. Many bad habits such as debauchery, alcoholism and drugs get fuelled with money.

One stands the risk of losing touch with the divinity when they are rich since they can become arrogant about their money.

> When the Gods received Hercules and entertained him at a banquet hosted by Jupiter, he responded courteously to the greetings of all, but when Plutus, the God of Wealth approached him, he cast his eyes upon the ground, turned away and pretended not to see him.
>
> Jupiter was surprised at this conduct and asked why, after having been so cordial with all the other Gods, he had behaved like that with Plutus.

'Sir,' said Hercules, 'I do not like Plutus, and I will tell you why. When we were on earth together, I always noticed that he was to be found in the company of scoundrels.'

Pleasure

Pleasure is so important for human beings that it is often equated with happiness. We enjoy tasty food and love visiting exotic places and admiring beautiful faces. We get pleasure from melodious music. But, the greatest pleasure a man derives is often from the fulfilment of his sensual desires.

These pleasant activities are also the greatest source of pain and suffering. Indulgence in food leads to obesity and several other diseases. Excessive consumption of food has become the primary reason of illness in people today.

Sex, which is another main source of joy for people, is also the source of greatest pain for them. Instances of rapes and crime against women are motivated by the desire of man to seek pleasure from sexual activities. Several men lose their wealth and honour due to their sexual adventurism.

Power

Power is highly valued and revered in the world. God is often called Almighty or Omnipotent as He is considered to be supremely powerful. The history of a nation is replete with tales of people in power in relevant times. Yet, power is also the greatest evil as it can corrupt human mind. Lord Acton, an English historian, writer and politician, once said, 'Power tends to corrupt, and absolute power corrupts absolutely. Great men are almost always bad men, even when they exercise influence and not authority.'

The quest of power can delude man. Power creates hatred and powerful people often fear for their lives. A man, when in power, can intimidate everyone but becomes scared for himself when out of power. Power is addictive; once you live and learn to wield power, it is difficult to live without it. You tend to create many enemies if you have been in power for a long time.

The Italian dictator, Benito Mussolini, was the most powerful man in Italy at a point of time and a key player in World War II. He was captured by partisans and executed, along with his mistress, Clara Petacci, at Mezzegra in 1945, and their bodies were hung at a gas station in a town square in Milan. According to Milan Radio, a woman fired five shots into Mussolini's body and shouted, 'Five shots for my five assassinated sons!' Other passers-by also spat on the dead bodies of the great dictator and his mistress.

We all aspire to rise in our organisations and become the boss. Yet the job of a boss is more difficult than that of the subordinates. Whenever he exercises power in his organisation, subordinates do not like it. If he becomes compassionate and easy-going with his subordinates, they take him for granted and the performance of the organisation may decline. A powerful person is hated by less-powerful people. Power often ends up becoming the greatest source of misery for many people.

Fame

One of the greatest desires of man is to become famous and well known. Famous people are always in the limelight; their presence enhances the prestige of any gathering. People wish to meet them, take their autographs, or have selfies clicked with them.

However, fame has its downside too. Famous people lose their privacy and are always under public critique. The miseries and failures of famous men are much more saleable than their successes. People love to gossip when celebrities fall from grace and leaders are caught in scandals.

Fred Allen, popular American comedian, once famously said, 'A celebrity is a person who works hard all his life to become well-known, then wears dark glasses to avoid being recognised.' Let's not forget the incident that led to Princess of Wales, Princess Diana's demise. She lost her life, in an accident, when her car was being chased by the paparazzi.

While people love to be famous, to fulfil their desire of being appreciated, they don't want to be cursed by the masses. A famous person becomes a captive of his own image and it is quite difficult for him to break the mould in which people have cast him. Kristen Stewart, Hollywood actor, said, 'The strangest part about being famous is you don't get to give first impressions anymore. Everyone already has an impression of you before you meet them.'

Often famous people become a commodity whose value is determined by the market condition based on demand and supply. When people want to know more about the celebrity, media sells their story after spicing it up. And if there is a decrease in the fan base, media forgets the same celebrity rather quickly.

> Once Churchill was asked by an admirer: 'Doesn't it thrill you, Mr Churchill, to know that every time you make a speech, the hall is packed to overflowing?'
>
> 'It is quite flattering,' Churchill replied. 'But whenever I feel this way I remember that if instead of making a political speech, I was being hanged, the crowd would be twice as big.'

Joy is Sorrow in Disguise

Buddha described life as suffering. Our sorrow is often hidden in our joy and vice versa. The famous writer Kahlil Gibran described the relationship between joy and sorrow as following:

> The deeper that sorrow carves into your being, the more joy you can contain.
>
> Is not the cup that holds your wine the very cup that was burned in the potter's oven?
>
> And is not the lute that soothes your spirit, the very wood that was hollowed with knives?
>
> When you are joyous, look deep into your heart and you shall find it is only that which has given you sorrow that is giving you joy.

> When you are sorrowful look again in your heart, and you shall see in truth that you are weeping for that which has been your delight.

The key to happiness is to use the source of happiness in the right quantity, at the right time and in the right way. There is nothing wrong per se with love, family, wealth, pleasure, power or fame. They are all necessary for happiness and living a good life. However, they become a source of problem, when we use them wrongly or in excess or at the wrong time.

Our happiness lies in using the right resources at the right time in the right way.

6

Comparison is Injurious to Happiness

Comparison is an act of violence against the self.

—Iyanla Vanzant, American inspirational speaker and life coach

Many people make their lives miserable by constantly comparing themselves with those who are better than them. Jack Canfield, an American author, motivational speaker and co-author of the *Chicken Soup for the Soul* series explains, 'I generally find that comparison is the fast track to unhappiness. No one ever compares themselves to someone else and comes out even. Nine times out of ten, we compare ourselves to people who are somehow better than us and end up feeling more inadequate.'

The fact is that everyone is better than every other person in some aspects and worse in others. You will have some things and will be missing out on others. Here is a story from Aesop's Fables explaining this simple truth.

> A donkey congratulated a horse for being taken care of so well, while he himself had scarcely enough to eat, and not even that without hard work. But when war broke out, the heavy-armed soldier mounted the horse and rushed into the very midst of the enemy, and the horse, got wounded and fell dead on the battle field.
>
> Then the donkey, seeing all these things, changed his mind, and commiserated with the horse, saying: 'How fortunate am I! I can remain at home in safety while he is exposed to all the perils of war.'

Why Comparison Brings Unhappiness?

Logically speaking, comparison should make at least one party happy. When two people are comparing themselves with each other, one who is better must feel happy. However, this hardly happens because we usually compare only those aspects of our existence where we are worse off and overlook the aspects where we are doing better. Nature has not given everything to everyone. If you have some qualities, you may also be lacking in some other aspects.

When we meet others, there is an instant comparison in our subconscious mind. People compare their looks, height, age, income, knowledge, qualification, spouse, children, profession, dresses, jewellery, etc. at the first sight or in the first meeting itself. It is impossible for any one person to be better than everyone else in all respects.

After each comparison, we can either feel happy in the knowledge that we are doing better than the other or choose to feel miserable at our comparative shortcomings. Most people get depressed by what they lack because pain is always more powerful than pleasure. If we have pain in one part of our body, we can't enjoy the good health of hundreds of other body parts.

Also, it is human tendency to take for granted what we have and crave for what we lack.

Often, the envious people, in order to make themselves feel better, focus their attention on the weaker points of the people who are superior to them and criticise them at every possible opportunity. They derive some sort of sadistic pleasure in demeaning their rivals or others who they think are at a more advantageous position than them. It is common for the older generation to criticise the younger generation, as in their unconscious mind they feel inadequate in comparison to them in several ways. The same tendency is also displayed by the younger people in respect to their seniors in age. Criticism of the poor by the rich and rich by the poor is another common quandary of every society.

However, such criticism doesn't improve our condition or make us happy. When we keep criticising others, it ultimately makes us feel even worse as our unconscious mind knows and accepts that the other person is better than us and we can't be like them.

When we compare ourselves with others, the pain of being inferior is usually more dominant than the pleasure of being a cut above. What can one do if someone else is taller, more gifted or blessed with better looks? This is something that can hardly be changed. One may be more qualified and more intelligent than the other person but such advantages seem of little value in comparison to what one lacks. Such pain can't be treated except by belittling the other person, which many people try to do by spreading malicious gossip or criticising. Dale Carnegie wrote in his classic book *How to Win Friends and Influence People*, 'Any fool can criticise, complain and condemn—and most fools do. But it takes character and self-control to be understanding and forgiving.'

Criticising and condemning others can't give anyone lasting happiness. Once people fall into the habit of criticising others, they become susceptible to even criticising their own selves as they too are not perfect. The habit of comparing leads to the habit of criticism, which soon leads to self-condemnation, and fills your life with pain and misery.

Learning to Appreciate

Instead of criticising people who are superior to you, learn from them and inculcate these superior qualities in your own life. Ralph Waldo Emerson, the famous American essayist and poet wisely said, 'In my walks, every man I meet is my superior in some way, and in that I learn from him.' If you develop the habit of learning from everyone and treat every better person as a teacher, you can be friends with everyone and become happier.

We must understand that each one of us is unique in this universe. Hence, it is pointless to compare ourselves with any other person. Just like a cow is not inferior to a dog, since both of them are perfect in themselves, we too are perfect in the way we are. We can make ourselves better and reach higher levels of perfection, but we can't become like anyone else.

Happy people never compare themselves with others as they are satisfied with what they have and what they are. They have a feeling of completeness as a human being. Once you are complete, you are peaceful and happy. The *Isha Upanishad* starts with this insightful verse:

Completeness is that, completeness is this,
From completeness, completeness comes forth.
Completeness from completeness taken away,
Completeness to completeness added,
Completeness alone remains.
Om. Peace! Peace! Peace!

When you are complete in yourself, you lack nothing. Hence, you don't need anything or anyone to complete yourself. If your stomach is full, you don't crave for food. Even if good food is offered to you, you will not be tempted. When you have slept peacefully through the night and your sleep is complete, you are less likely to wake up tired in the morning or wanting to sleep more. When you are happy in your job, you don't feel the need to compare yourself with anyone else.

People compare because they feel incomplete and unfulfilled. If their desire to complete themselves is not satisfied for long, it becomes a craving that disturbs all their joy. If we understand our sense of completeness thoroughly, we can also understand what we can't be (we can't organically become a woman, if born a man) and hence we won't lose happiness chasing the impossible. If there is anything that you find inadequate and you can make it up, you should go ahead and make yourself more complete and become a more fulfilled person.

A happy person does not compare with others but feels blessed with what he has. His focus is on the achievement of self and not on what others have achieved. If others are better than him, he is happy to be a friend to them and be proud of their successes. If some people are not as good as him, he helps them to improve.

A happy person compares only with self. He tries to be a better person than what he had been yesterday. He tries to help everyone to become better than what they are rather than pulling them down to satisfy his own sense of misplaced superiority. He has no desire of making others miserable by berating them and destroying their happiness.

When you harm others, you expose yourself to similar harm, when others try to get even. Similarly, when you help others, you get help back in most natural ways without even asking. The world is like a mirror that reflects our own image to us in the truest way.

If you wish to be happy, develop the habit of appreciation rather than comparison. Whenever you find a better person, appreciate him not only to his face but even in the presence of others. This will make you a better person because what we admire, we become. A truly happy person always tries to create a better and more complete world and increases the happiness quotient of the world.

7

Lying Leads to Unhappiness

For every good reason there is to lie, there is a better reason to tell the truth.

—Bo Bennett, American author

Truth is often compared with God. Truth is liberating. Jesus Christ said, 'If you abide in My word, you are My disciples indeed. And you shall know the truth, and the truth shall make you free.'(*John 8:31b-32 NKJV*). On the other hand, a single lie can destroy your reputation forever when it gets discovered. Even if you are telling the truth, people stop believing you, if you develop the reputation of being a liar.

However, many people are tempted to lie because a lie provides instant gratification.

> On a Friday afternoon, a young man walked into a jewellery shop with a beautiful young woman.
>
> The girl selected a magnificent necklace.

The man said to the jeweller, 'We are going out of town for the weekend and will be back to pick it up on Monday.'

The couple left the store.

On Monday, the young man came to the shop and said to the jeweller, 'I did not want to purchase that necklace. I have come to sincerely thank you for helping me have a really wonderful weekend.'

It is, therefore, common for people to lie for instant gratification. Lying is even considered to be an art in certain professions such as marketing, politics, advertising or when working as a lawyer. If you develop the habit of lying, you may start to find it difficult to speak the truth.

But, lies can provide only instant gratification and not long-term benefits. They provide only temporary relief from pain. People, who lie frequently, soon may not even remember what lies they said before whom. They are always scared of their lies getting exposed. And once a lie is exposed, all credibility and reputation of the person gets lost in the eyes of not only the person to whom the lie was spoken to, but also before others, because people who get cheated start talking ill about the liar. A liar can hardly experience happiness as he is constantly worried about getting caught and exposed. He is, therefore, constantly fabricating another set of lies to justify his earlier lies.

Why Do People Lie?

Adolf Hitler once said, 'If you tell a big enough lie and tell it frequently enough, it will be believed.' People lie to get some immediate advantage accruing from lying.

- Salesmen lie to sell their goods and services.
- Politicians lie to get votes.
- Lovers lie to impress their beloved.
- Parents lie to avoid answering inconvenient questions of their children.
- Children lie to their parents to cover up their mischiefs.

When lying becomes epidemic in a profession, an honest person finds it difficult to survive in the same. This spoils the image of the whole profession as people stop trusting everyone related to that line of work. Politicians are notorious for making false promises to win the votes of people. They suffer loss of respect in the society when they fail to deliver on their promises. People judge politicians not for what they have done, but for what they have failed to deliver on their promises. Opposition parties keep reminding people of the promises made by the politician, and ensure that the public never forgets the same. In order to explain their failure in the deliverance of the promises, the politician has to speak even more lies.

> Once Winston Churchill was asked, 'What qualities does a politician require?'
>
> He replied promptly, 'The ability to foretell what is going to happen tomorrow, next week, next month, and next year.'
>
> He then paused for a moment and continued, 'And to have the ability afterwards to explain why it didn't happen.'

Politics has acquired such a bad reputation in many parts of the world that good people don't want to join politics or associate themselves with politicians anymore.

Often clever businessmen also resort to covert ways of lying in order to boost the sales of their products—they do so through false and deceptive advertising.

Some professions, like that of law, are today identified with lying to an extent that they have lost their reputation. People in such professions can't enjoy true happiness even if they are rich and successful. A lawyer often knows that his client has committed a murder, rape or theft and yet he chooses to defend him in the court and prove him innocent. He deliberately twists the facts and circumstances of the case to win the case. These professionals can make great amounts of money defending the guilty but they suffer due to their conscience.

> A lawyer and an engineer were fishing in the Caribbean when they got talking. The lawyer mentioned, 'I'm here because my house burned down and everything got destroyed. The insurance company paid for everything.'
>
> 'That's quite a coincidence,' remarked the engineer, 'I'm here because my house and all my belongings were destroyed by a flood. My insurance company, too, paid for everything.'
>
> There was a brief pause, and then the puzzled lawyer asked, 'How do you start a flood?'

While most people would be willing to ignore lies that are spoken in discharging their professional duties, they are less forgiving when it comes to personal relationships. Most people are hurt when they come to know that their loved ones were cheating on them. It is difficult to forgive the lies of those whom we love and trust. A lie of a politician, businessman or a lawyer is not so painful since we never trusted them in the first place. But we can't accept the lies of our close friends and family members, if we ourselves have been honest with them.

The habit of lying kills our happiness slowly but surely. A dishonest person is rarely happy. When no one trusts you, it becomes impossible to build relationships and be loved. When you are unloved and disconnected with humanity, how can you be happy?

Honesty is the Best Policy

If lying is detrimental to happiness, honesty is conducive to it. Thomas Jefferson, the American founding father and the principal author of the *Declaration of Independence* and the third President of the United States, wisely said, 'Honesty is the first chapter in the book of wisdom.'

All virtues of a man rest upon his honesty and integrity; if you are not honest, you can't sustain any other virtue. While honesty may not provide you any instant benefit, it prepares you for the challenges of life. If you are honest, your conscience is clear. And the road to everlasting happiness goes through a clear conscience.

8

Manage Your Failures

You cannot climb the ladder of success dressed in the costume of failure.

—Zig Ziglar, American author and motivational speaker

One of the major trends, nowadays, among the youth is to follow your passion and your dream. Democracy has given equal rights to all citizens of the nation and everyone in the society can aspire to become anything. When there is no limit on aspirations, people dream of the greatest things in the world. Hence, many can harbour the dream of becoming the President or Prime Minister, film stars, writers, music directors, the richest businessman or a top sports personality.

As there are only a few slots available on the top, most people end up failing to realise their dreams and becoming partial or total failures in their mission. The higher their goal, the more is the competition and greater the chances of failure.

It is for this reason that failure has become all pervasive in the modern world. Misery in the modern world is not because people don't have food to eat or a house to live. They are unhappy because they have failed to realise their dreams. And this failure has been all the more accentuated with the advent of social media in our lives, where we are hyper connected with everyone else—the success of our friends, colleagues and relatives is on display in a more pompous manner than before and is tempting us to compare ourselves continuously and feel even more low. Failures are always painful and give rise to unhappiness.

Why People Fail?

'It is impossible to live without failing at something', JK Rowling said. She adds, 'Unless you live so cautiously that you might as well not have lived at all, in which case you have failed by default.' Failure is a part of our struggle for success. When we are trying to achieve something great, we must prepare ourselves to fail. The higher our aspiration, the greater are our chances of failure.

Let's explain this with an example.

Suppose you are trying to become a high-jumper. The present world record for high jump is around 2.45 metres.

If you keep your goal at merely one metre, you can perhaps easily jump this height. As you successfully jump that height, you keep increasing the bar bit by bit from one metre to 2.5 metres.

Gradually you would notice that your failure rate starts increasing.

The higher is your target, the more difficult it is to achieve success in your endeavour.

You would soon notice that despite all your efforts, you are not able to cross a particular height, however hard you try.

If you don't moderate your goal according to your ability, you would be failing 100 per cent time.

If you fail all the time, how can you enjoy any happiness?

One way to increase your happiness is thus to reduce your failure rate by reducing your goals.

If you keep your goals too easy, you can achieve 100 per cent success, but you would not be able to make the best use of your potential.

The right approach of life is, therefore, to neither keep your goals too low nor too high but find an optimum point so that your successes and failures are balanced in the right proportion.

Importance of Success

Every success makes us happy and every failure gives us pain. When you succeed, it is a reflection of your superior understanding of the self and the circumstances. But it is important to note that one can't succeed in life just because another person has succeeded earlier (if an Olympic-level athlete can do something, so can I). One can only taste success by being realistic about one's own abilities and choosing the right assignment.

Perseverance does not pay when you are attempting something unrealistic. You must learn from your failures, your limitations and focus, and improve on the areas where you can perform better and succeed frequently.

Albert Schweitzer, a theologian and philosopher once said: 'Success is not the key to happiness. Happiness is the key to success. If you love what you are doing, you will be successful.' This statement holds true because when you know you are going to be successful, you are likely to be happy executing that job. There is no way you can force yourself to be happy, if the chances of failure are very high in your endeavours.

Instead of arguing whether happiness gives one success or success makes one happy, we may agree that happiness and success are interconnected with each other and are the cause and effect of each other. Similarly, failure and unhappiness are also cause and effect of each other.

We can consider successes and failures in our life as credit and debit entries of our happiness account. Every time we succeed in achieving our goal, we get credit in the form of happiness and every time we fail, we debit our happiness account. If we have enough credits of happiness, we can easily withstand some failures just like the person who has a million dollar bank balance, does not get disconcerted if he loses out on a few thousand dollars. However, the same loss can bring much grief to a person who has a very small balance in his account.

Avoiding Failures

We can either increase our 'happiness account balance' by depositing more success into it or by minimising the withdrawals by lowering instances of failures. As mentioned earlier, the possible way to maintain this balance is to know and accept your own limitations, be realistic, and remember that there are many others in the world who also are equally, if not more, talented.

- You may be a good artist but still not so good that you can make a mark as a world-class artist
- You may be good at writing but not good enough to be a renowned writer

While routine and mundane jobs may be ridiculed or looked down upon in some circles, the fact is that these jobs provide livelihood to millions of people. A good information technology company in India employs thousands of professionals every year giving them decent salaries. However, in fields such as politics, writing, cinema or arts, there are very few people who come on top, and those who do, end up taking home almost all the rewards, leaving little for the runners-up or the bottom rankers.

Hence, it would be better to pursue a profession which can, at least, bring a decent living than trying to earn living in a profession, which is out of limits for you and your skill set. In such well-known professions, the top few may be making enormous amounts of money and hogging all the limelight but virtually nothing is left for those who are at the bottom of the pyramid.

Once you have secured yourself a source of steady income, you can then try your hands at a profession in the area of your talent.

Balancing Success and Failures

The key to leading a happy life is to strike an appropriate balance between your successes and failures. It may be prudent to be realistic about your aspirations.

- If you aim too high, you increase the chances of failure and hence suffering.
- If you try too low, your success rate may go up but your growth will be stunted.

The right approach is to be able to aim high enough that will bring success as well as failure. While risk-taking is good if experimented at a lower scale, risk-taking at the highest level is like burning-the-boat, that is, to have either everything or nothing, which may lead to massive disruptions in your life.

It is equally unwise to only seek success, skirting all chances of failure akin to a man who only deposits in his bank account but never withdraws from it. The deposit makes sense only if you intend to withdraw it at an appropriate time. An 'only-deposit' account is of no use to the depositor.

It is, therefore, important to have a judicious balance of success and failure. A little failure, can, in fact, multiply the joy of success manifold. Remember the words of Winston Churchill: 'Success is not final, failure is not fatal: it is the courage to continue that counts.'

Learning from Failures

Failure may even be useful in the path of success and happiness, if we learn the lessons from our failures and use such lessons to improve our chances of success. We are often told that Thomas A Edison failed 10,000 times before he could invent the electric bulb. We also know that he did not consider it as failure as he said, 'I have not failed. I've just found 10,000 ways that won't work.' However, it is not easy to keep your spirit high after failing 10,000 times. Edison had many creative accomplishments to his credit to be able to live with some of his failures. You have to be as positive and intelligent as Edison to fail 10,000 times and still feel excited even amidst your failures. What worked for Edison may not work for everyone.

You can't succeed when you imitate someone else. Everyone can't be Thomas Edison or Albert Einstein. When you imitate someone else, without understanding your own talents or limitations, the chances of failure increase. It would be better to lower your expectations to an extent that successes start pouring more frequently in your life to mitigate the pain accruing from failures. However, when success becomes a norm and the memories of failure start to fade, it is then the time to raise the bar and take up newer challenges in life, or add more skills to your own skill set. While failure is important for success, take only as much failures as you can afford to, without losing all your happiness. Failing more than what you can withstand is a recipe for suffering.

9

Earn Honestly, Spend Wisely

In a country well governed, poverty is something to be ashamed of. In a country badly governed, wealth is something to be ashamed of.

—Confucius

Wealth has been criticised and ridiculed by the intellectuals and saints. It has even been called the root of all evil.

The Bible also considers wealth as an adversary of God: 'No one can serve two masters. Either you will hate one and love the other, or you will be devoted to one and despise the other. You cannot serve both God and money.' (*Luke 16:13 NIV*)

The criticism of wealth and glorification of poverty is a popular rhetoric because most people are not rich and they feel comforted in their lack of wealth when wealth is associated with evil. Many continue to believe in the futility of wealth till they acquire the wisdom to know what is good for them.

> An angel appears at a faculty meeting and tells the dean that in return for his unselfish and exemplary behaviour, the Lord will reward him with his choice of infinite wealth, wisdom or beauty.
>
> Without hesitating, the dean selects infinite wisdom.
>
> 'Done!' says the angel and disappears in a cloud of smoke and a bolt of lightning.
>
> Now, all heads turn towards the dean, who sits surrounded by a faint halo of light. One of his colleagues whispers, 'Say something.'
>
> The dean sighs and says, 'I should have taken the money.'

The Importance of Wealth

The importance of wealth is well known. You need money to buy everything that is required for your survival. It is impossible to live an honourable life if you are poor. No self-respecting human being would like to beg from another human being for food, water and shelter. Those who live on alms can hardly expect respect in the society.

Wealth is like food. You can't survive in this world without wealth just like your body can't survive without food. More wealth, however, does not mean more happiness just like more food does not mean better health. Most people in the modern world are making their lives miserable not because they have no food, but because they eat excessively. The same goes for wealth. We must know how much wealth is needed to live a decent life and be happy.

Making money should not be the purpose of our living but only means to achieve our purpose. You must eat to live and not live to eat. Jesus Christ expounded, 'Man does not live by bread alone.'

If you wish to know the importance of food, ask a hungry man and not the one who has never known hunger in his life. You can understand the importance of wealth by imagining yourself without money. Just like a man who faces hunger too frequently can't be healthy, a poor man struggling for basic necessities too can't be really happy in life.

Wealth is necessary for your physical survival. If you have accumulated sufficient wealth, you get secured for future as you don't have to worry about the fulfilment of your basic needs. A wealthy person also enjoys respectable status in the society because wealth is an indication of worldly success. Wealth also gives you power to help others by supplying your material needs and making your life more joyful.

Yet, you can't legitimately earn wealth unless you have something to contribute to the society. You have to give something to the world in order to earn wealth. You, then, spend wealth to get what you need.

Our happiness from wealth, thus, depends on how we earn money and how we spend it.

Working with Joy

It is never easy to earn wealth. We give almost half of our waking hours to earn sufficient money to take care of the needs of self and our family. Most people don't like what they do but do it anyway for the sake of money.

Life is a torture if you have to do what you don't like. Johnny Carson, an American television host, comedian, writer, producer and musician advised, 'Never continue in a job you don't enjoy. If you're happy in what you're doing, you'll like yourself, you'll have inner peace. And if you have that, along with physical health, you will have had more success than you could possibly have imagined.'

Kahlil Gibran said in one of his works, 'Work is love made visible. And if you cannot work with love but only with distaste, it is better that you should leave your work and sit at the gate of the temple and take alms of those who work with joy.'

If you hate what you do, you may be losing more than what you are earning not just in terms of money. You earn your wealth by spending not only your physical energies, but also your mental, emotional and spiritual energies. You utilise and exhaust your energies when dealing with your bosses, subordinates, colleagues, workers or customers. When you are dealing with people whom you don't know or whom you don't like, or for a job which you abhor, your emotional energies are drained faster. When you are faking a smile or praising someone against your will, you are again getting emotionally drained out.

There is a loss or gain of spiritual energies when you are performing your job. When you are doing something for the betterment of the world, you gain spiritual energy because your conscience becomes stronger with every act. When you are working contrary to the interests of the world, you lose spiritual energy and your conscience becomes weaker by every such act. Certain trades such as human trafficking, drug peddling, arms and/or liquor sales cause harm to the world and hence these trades cast a burden on your conscience. You remain a loser when you are in these professions irrespective of the wealth you make. Bible says, 'What good is it for someone to gain the whole world, and yet lose or forfeit their very self?' (*Luke 9:25 NIV*)

While wealth is important, you must understand the physical, mental, emotional and spiritual cost of earning it. Confucius once said, 'Choose a job you love, and you will never have to work a day in your life.' Such a job may not give you the best pay, but it would surely give you the greatest joy since you love doing it. When you love your job, the quality of work improves effortlessly. You don't get tired with your work but feel recharged. Your work itself becomes a great source of joy for you.

Joy of Spending

You don't earn money to stow away in safety lockers in a bank. You earn money so that you can spend it to fulfil your needs, aspirations and desires. Your happiness depends not only on how you earn money but also on how you spend it. The methods of earning and spending are intimately connected with each other.

- A person who earns his money honestly can't spend it on immoral pursuits.
- A person who earns his money dishonestly often wastes it on immoral pursuits.

If you have earned money by doing the work you love, you don't feel the need to buy your joys and pleasures with your income since your job itself is a source of joy for you. American author Stephen King accepted this with pride: 'Yes, I've made a great deal of dough from my fiction, but I never set a single word down on paper with the thought of being paid for it…I have written because it fulfilled me…I did it for the buzz. I did it for the pure joy of the thing. And if you can do it for joy, you can do it forever.'

On the contrary, when you are earning money by doing what you don't particularly like, there will be an urgent need to buy pleasure and happiness, from the acquired money to justify the pain and suffering you are going through in your work. The more is the suffering in earning the wealth, the greater is the desire of enjoying pleasure from the money so earned. If we spend our wealth carefully and optimally, our need to earn money is considerably reduced and we have much more time at our disposal to live our life the way we want to. We can choose professions that we love. If our profession is in tune with our nature, it gives us joy even if the remuneration is less.

We discover ourselves by doing what we love. The famous Sufi poet Rumi said, 'Everyone has been made for some particular work, and the desire for that work has been put in every heart.'

When we do what we love to do, we give our best and we soon achieve perfection. Such a person enjoys tremendous joy in his work and also earns sufficient money to enjoy his leisure. He can fill every corner of his life with happiness.

Some people who win huge money in lottery or through inheritance lose it too if they don't spend it judiciously.

- If you spend your money in consuming harmful foods and drinks, the fault is in you and not in the money.
- If you spend your money on alcohol, drugs and other intoxicants and, thus, spoil your health and character, it is foolish to blame money for it.
- If you waste your wealth imprudently in your relationships, the fault is yours and not of your wealth.

Wealth is one of the most important sources of happiness. It becomes a source of pain only when we earn or spend it inappropriately.

10

Ignorance is a Curse

Ignorance is the curse of God; knowledge is the wing wherewith we fly to heaven.

—William Shakespeare

Siddhartha Gautam was the son of Suddhodana, the king of Lumbini in Nepal. His father wished him to be a great king. Gautam was provided with all the luxuries of life and married at the age of sixteen. Soon, he was blessed with a son. Gautam's father ensured that his son did not see any human suffering. Hence, he was totally ignorant of the afflictions of human beings.

One day, at the age of twenty-nine years, Gautam went out of his palace to see his subjects. On the way, he saw an old man, a sick man, a deceased man and an ascetic. When he asked his charioteer the significance of these people, he was told that everyone gets old, falls sick and eventually dies. Gautam got depressed looking at the sufferings of human beings and left his palace and family to become an ascetic and search the Truth which would remove the sufferings of mankind. After more than five years in his quest, he got enlightened and became the Buddha—'The Enlightened One'.

We see these four types of people around us all the time, but we learn no lesson. Newton discovered the principles of gravity by observing the fall of an apple from a tree. Billions of people before him would have seen fruits falling on the ground, from trees, but failed to understand the significance of such incidents and failed to discover the laws that govern our lives. When we keep ignoring what is happening around us, we remain ignorant.

The word 'ignorance' comes from the Latin root *ignorans*, meaning 'to ignore'. Ignorance means lack of knowledge, education, learning and information.

Even if you have never gone to school or read a single book, you can still be knowledgeable if you don't ignore what is happening around you.

You can't shed ignorance unless you develop the habit to learn by observation and self-analysis. A man who has mastered all the books in the world may still be ignorant if he fails to connect this bookish knowledge with the real world.

We can't know everything. Yet if we know 'how to learn', we can learn what we need to know to live our lives well. Benjamin Franklin once said, 'Being ignorant is not so much a shame, as being unwilling to learn.'

We often miss out the cues to learn something from real-life incidents that occur around us and even from what we see with our own eyes. We prefer to follow the teachings of great men without understanding the true meaning of their words.

The Enlightenment of Buddha

Buddha attained enlightenment after he closely observed the real world and learnt the valuable lessons himself. We remain ignorant because we choose to ignore the importance of the four things responsible for the enlightenment of Buddha. Let's closely understand these four truths of life.

1. **Illness:** It is common to fall sick. However, we never fall sick without a reason. Every illness has a reason, and we can prevent illness by knowing the causes of it. Sometimes people get into the habit of smoking, drinking or overeating which is harmful to their health or at other times, they are careless about hygiene. Is it not a wonder they still hope that they would never be affected by their deeds? If only you pay attention to what makes you ill and are able to visualise the pain you suffer once afflicted by the illness, you can take precautions and reduce your chances of falling sick.
2. **Old Age:** Most people behave as if they are never going to get old. As we grow older, we pay for everything we did in our youth. If you mistreat your body at a young age, you pay heavily

when you get old. If you mistreat your children, friends and relatives, you suffer from their lack of affection, care and sympathy at old age. When you cheat the society, defraud the government and commit immoral acts, you are confined in prison or boycotted by the society at the latter age. As you sow at young age, so shall you reap at old age.

3. **Death:** Who can ignore the fact that we all have limited lifespans? Yet people keep on accumulating wealth and doing selfish acts as if they are going to live forever. You can't carry anything away from this world when you die. If only you can remember that you have to die one day, you will live life more meaningfully and ethically.
4. **Ascetic:** The fourth person whom Buddha saw was an ascetic or a monk, who had no wealth or possessions. An ascetic survives only on alms. For a common man, this is possibly the most difficult way of living. Yet an ascetic is no less happy than the other rational and rich, worldly people. We can learn from an ascetic that we don't need great wealth to be happy. Therefore, cease to strive accumulating too much of wealth in an attempt to live happily.

Distortion of Truth

'The greatest enemy of knowledge is not ignorance, it is the illusion of knowledge,' wrote Daniel J Boorstin in his book, *The Discoverers: A History of Man's Search to Know*

His World and Himself. Many people are ignorant not because they don't know much but because they have accumulated false or worthless knowledge.

We are bombarded with information from all sides—through the internet, electronic and social media. However, much of such information is untrue or irrelevant. There is some truth in the words of Cara Stein, the author of *Happiness: 10 Simple Tools to a Happier Life!*:

> In case you don't already know, the main purpose of television, magazines, newspapers and all popular media is to sell advertisements. That's how they make money. They produce content to get your attention so you'll see as many of their ads as possible.

When you are unhappy with your life, you look for happiness outside and often end up buying products that claim to bring happiness to your life. Hence, the media is more interested in highlighting negativity that makes us unhappy, rather than showing us the content, which may bring joy and hope to people.

If you are happy, you may not be tempted to buy anything except the real necessities of life. Businesses, therefore, exaggerate negativities in the world to sell their products and services. They try to convince you that if you wish to be happy, you must buy their car, home or clothes or visit the exotic locations managed by them.

Many people in modern times are developing distorted vision of life as they are spending more time in the 'virtual world' than in the 'real world'. People are developing 'availability bias' due to excessive absorption of the content that is untrue, half-true, misleading or just fiction. Those who spend more time on the internet and electronic media are more likely to see more negativity in the world than what it really is. We all wish to see goodness in this world. The wide gap between what 'is available' and what 'should be' creates confusion, pain, fear and contempt.

If you wish to be happy, you have to develop the right vision to discover the positivity in the world through your own efforts. Only then can you create an accurate picture of the world in your mind and know the complete truth.

When you try to buy happiness through money, you are trapped in a vicious circle. You have to slog longer to make more money to buy the 'elements of happiness' advertised by big businesses. You thus make your life even more miserable in the process. These clever corporations always come up with newer and more expensive products to make you discard your existing possessions and keep buying their new products and add money to their bank accounts.

Developing the Illusion of Knowledge

George Bernard Shaw said, 'Beware of false knowledge; it is more dangerous than ignorance.' False knowledge is the real form of ignorance in modern times. You have to remove all illusionary knowledge to understand the reality.

True knowledge is one that comes from within, from personal experiences, or from a reliable source. True knowledge is same all over the world and for everyone.

However, it is not easy to acquire true knowledge because you have to learn it only by personal effort and make it part of your life through personal experiences. Most people wish to avoid the hard work or the pain of learning through experience and hence prefer to follow the 'second-hand knowledge' available without ever testing its credibility themselves. Thus, they remain ignorant despite having large amount of second-hand knowledge accumulated by them in their lifetime.

We often create our worldview based on movies and fictions books, which are actually drafted to entertain us and make us forget reality for a short time. A practical purpose behind any movie is to fill the coffers of the producers, actors and other professionals and not to show the reality which we see around us all the time, free of cost. When you start believing the characters of the movies to be real, you are bound to be frustrated because the real world and its people are always so different and so inadequate as compared to the heroes and heroines in the movies.

When we make our ideals based on fiction and expect the world to fit into the moulds of those ideals, we get frustrated because different people have different ideals. Every person chooses his ideal on the basis of what suits him the most.

The ideals of a poor man are different from those of a rich man. For example, a poor man would like wealth to be distributed evenly while a rich man would favour rewards based on outcomes.

Interestingly, for every ideal there is an opposite one. Hence, to expect everyone to follow your ideal is a sure shot recipe to frustration, conflict and unhappiness.

Some people get highly motivated after reading an inspirational book or listening to a motivational speaker and start believing the words they read or hear as true knowledge. Most motivational speakers typically use anecdotes rather than statistics to prove their point. They don't speak about the thousands of failures of millions of hapless men and women but always tell the story of one successful person to prove their point. They make great promises akin to a good salesman out to sell his wares. Many people follow their advice and unfortunately discover that they still are not able to achieve the promised success.

How can it be otherwise?

If there are a thousand applicants for one post and only one is to be selected, the other applicants have to fail, howsoever motivated and positive they may be.

It is your job to get the hard facts right to grasp the truth totally. It is better to build inner strength and try inside-out approach rather than using quick fixes suggested by experts in the business of selling fallacy in the guise of truth, hope and positive thinking.

The Curse of Ignorance

Ignorance is not a bliss but a curse. Ignorance is like darkness while knowledge is like a ray of light. It is foolish to think that a blind man's life is better than that of a person who is blessed with two perfect eyes. You can't convert day into night by simply closing your eyes. By ignoring the thoughts of death, you don't become immortal. The reality is going to haunt you whether you like it or not. Aldous Huxley, English writer and philosopher, warned us, 'Facts do not cease to exist because they are ignored.'

The world is governed by many eternal laws. These laws work irrespective of whether you know them or not.

When we end up creating wrong models of the world based on incorrect laws of human behaviour, the world doesn't change its laws to accommodate our ignorance. The ignorant people, therefore, feel quite unhappy when the world does not fit into their worldview and act according to their ideas and concepts.

- When we are ignorant, we see the world from our point of view and expect the world to behave according to our perception.
- When we are wise, we see ourselves as part of the world, and we try to fit into the world.

When our ignorance is eliminated, we see the reality as it is and that is the beginning of living a life of awareness and joy.

11

Be the Master of Law

There is no greater tyranny than that which is perpetrated under the shield of the law and in the name of justice.

—Charles de Montesquieu, French judge and political philosopher

In his 1977 judgment in the case of *Gouriet vs Union of Post Office Workers and Others,* Lord Denning, the most celebrated English judge of the twentieth century spoke these famous words: 'Be you ever so high, the law is above you'. The message of the superiority of the written law has become the most celebrated dictum in the law books and in almost every civilised country. It is quoted frequently by the judges worldwide.

When law is above everyone, what is the status of the human beings?

Have men become slaves to law?

All laws are inherently subjective. They are neither created in heaven nor are they sacrosanct. They change with time, place and circumstances. Laws are made to protect the interest of those who are in power. In democratic countries, the majority of the people rule the country through their elected representatives. John Stuart Mill, British philosopher and economist, argued in his famous 1859 book *On Liberty*, that democracy often results in oppression of minority groups. He called this 'tyranny of the majority' (or tyranny of the masses). He explained this as being an inherent weakness of direct democracy and majority rule in which the majority of an electorate can and does place its own interests above, and at the expense of those in the minority.

It has, therefore, become common to find the law in a democratic country awarding undue favour to classes and castes of people who are in majority as they possess the power to numbers during elections.

More than two thousand years ago, Jesus Christ was crucified by the Jews according to the law prevalent at that time. Even before Jesus Christ, Socrates was punished to death by being forced to drink poison, according to the law of the time. In modern times, we have seen the imprisonment of Mahatma Gandhi and Nelson Mandela according to laws framed by the ruling governments.

When time changes, the law also changes to suit the new rulers. Often the same people who were being accused of heinous crimes like treason according to the then laws, become the martyrs and messiahs when the laws are changed. Mahatma Gandhi is now considered to be the 'Father of the Nation' for India, while he was imprisoned repeatedly on sedition charges during the British rule.

It is erroneous to assume that laws are sacrosanct and everyone should follow them. The State expects its citizens to comply with the laws unconditionally. But when a lot of people don't follow the laws, people believing in the sanctity of laws also become quite unhappy with the way things are. But, they may not be even happy with themselves because they themselves can't obey all the laws.

The Subjectivity of Laws

Every law restricts freedom of its people. Every law imposes additional responsibility or tax on the citizens. An American politician, Gideon J Tucker aptly said 'No man's life, liberty or property is safe while the Legislature is in session.'

All laws are subjective and can benefit a few while harm others. Laws are like medicines made to cure a disease of the society at some point of time. Most laws, like most allopathic medicines, have some side effects and worsen the ailment if used wrongly. Sometimes, they worsen the situation because, through forceful disciplining, they suppress the natural power of a society to self-heal. Laws often become as addictive to a society as drugs are to a repeated user.

Thereafter, even more laws are drafted to overcome the ailments of the society. Newer laws create further complications and the cycle continues. Today, we have so many laws in a civilised country that even the governments have lost count of them. Yet people have not become more law-abiding than their ancestors. Today, laws are twisted, turned and broken more than ever before.

Can you live a healthy life by taking hundreds of medicines every day?

You may need aspirin to treat pain and to reduce fever or inflammation. However, once your pain and fever have gone, you must immediately stop its consumption, because if you continue to take aspirin like a daily dose of food, it may become poison for you. It loses all its curative powers once you are healthy and may lead to side effects such as swelling of face, upset stomach, heartburn or headache, if consumed without a need and over a period of time.

All modern societies in the world are suffering from side effects of thousands of laws forced upon them since time immemorial. Unfortunately, these laws are implemented uniformly on all people whether they are suffering from any ailment or not. Uniform application of laws may be as dangerous as administering all prescribed medicines to every person in a society irrespective of his health condition.

The Slavery of Law

There are two types of laws that are broadly used to govern societies. The first are the laws of the scriptures (religious or moral laws) and the second are the laws of legislatures (statute laws). While religious people consider the religious laws sacrosanct, the secularists worship the statute laws with same reverence. When people find that others are not followings these laws, they become unhappy and angry.

If you decide to follow all laws of your country and society, you will end up making yourself miserable like a slave owned by several thousand masters.

I am not trying to suggest that you must not follow the laws of the land. However, you should treat laws as necessary evils and not as Gospel Truths.

Wise people treat laws as guidelines, issued by the society and they understand that observance of these laws is the price that they are paying to live in a civilised society.

A friend of mine was once arguing about the problem of stray dogs in India. He lamented that these dogs bite people, litter the roads and create nuisance in the city. With great admiration, he referred to a friend who had secretly killed more than three thousand dogs one by one. He strongly held the view that all stray dogs must be killed by passing a law in the Parliament.

However, there may be a counter view against such a law.

- Earth does not belong only to the human race.
- Other species created by nature have an equal right to live.
- Man has no moral right to kill a breed of species just because it is not useful to him.

Would you be willing to commit genocide by killing an entire population of people belonging to a race or religion just because a few of them harmed another person?

Many countries have legalised culling of stray animals by passing a law in this regard, but in other countries, it may be an offence to kill dogs and may invite punishment.

Either way the law is made, it would be unacceptable for people with a different perspective of life.

Laws of Scriptures

One of the most fundamental laws of Bible is: 'Do not resist an evil person. If anyone slaps you on the right cheek, turn to them the other cheek also. And if anyone wants to sue you and take your shirt, hand over your coat as well.'

We know from our experience that it is impossible to live life by following this diktat. If you decide to abide by this law, chances are that you will be looted off all your property and belongings and even be thrown out of your house to starve to death. Hence, we also have a law that contradicts this law in the Bible itself. The opposite of 'offer your other cheek' principle is an 'eye-for-eye' policy mentioned in the Bible where God says: 'If there is serious injury, you are to take life for life, eye for eye, tooth for tooth, hand for hand, foot for foot, burn for burn, wound for wound, bruise for bruise.'

Even if the 'eye-for-eye' law looks barbarian to civilised people, most people, in their hearts, want to follow the 'eye-for-eye' policy against those who hurt them.

The bottom line is that no law is beneficial in all conditions. You can't apply 'eye-for-eye' policy if your opponent is way stronger than you.

Timur's armies were plundering the entire Central Asia and rumours were that Timur was next headed for Mullah's village. Hearing this, Mullah in his Friday sermon called for a collective prayer. 'Let us all pray for the death of Timur the Lame before he comes.'

All the villagers said 'Amen' loudly.

A man stood up from among the worshippers and asked, 'Have you ever seen Timur?'

Mullah replied, 'No, and I have not seen you before either.'

The man said, 'You are right, because I am Timur.'

Mullah was stunned by the news, and so were all the villagers. Mullah calmly resumed his sermon. 'Let us pray once more collectively, this time for our *janazah* (funeral prayer).'

'How can you pray for your own *janazah*, you fool,' asked Timur, '*janazah* is prayed by the living for the dead.'

'Yes my lord, but you see,' replied Mullah, 'we are all about to be dead with no one to pray *janazah* on us. So we have to take care of our *janazah* ourselves.'

Timur laughed his heart out and pardoned Mullah.

You don't shout back when your boss reprimands you. 'Eye-for-eye' policy works well when you are stronger than the one who has hurt you. When your opponent is more powerful than you, 'offer your other cheek' law often works better. Mahatma Gandhi used this policy against British rule and was able to get independence for India.

People follow law when it is beneficial for them and disobey it when it is against them. For example, the laws of caste-based reservation or positive discrimination look perfectly logical and justified to people who are benefited by such policies but seem quite unfair and unjust to those who lose opportunities due to these laws. There is no way you can bridge the gap as every rule will restrict the benefits for someone and give it away to another person against the wishes of the former. If the benefit could have been passed on voluntarily, there would have been no need of law at all.

People, who want everyone to follow the laws favourable to them, are unhappy because others may not prefer the same law. Others may in turn expect the same from the first lot of people in respect to the laws that favour them, even though the law might be depriving the first set of people of some advantage.

A happy person uses the law merely as guidelines and tries to live life according to his own set of rules without harming others. A happy person does not see the world as imperfect as he knows that the world has always been like that and it shall always continue to be the same. He finds the world as perfect as it could be. Robert Browning wrote beautifully.

The year's at the spring
And day's at the morn;
Morning's at seven;
The hillside's dew-pearled;
The lark's on the wing;
The snail's on the thorn:

God's in His heaven—
All's right with the world!

While an unhappy person is always miserable because his attention is focused on the imperfections of the world where most people are not law-abiding, a wise person is joyful because his focus is on the perfection of the world. Your faith in the rules and laws of your country or your religion is what makes you think that the world is imperfect. Happy people know that all the imperfections of the world are due to the conditioning of our minds which seeks perfection in the world according to the moral and statuary laws. Unless you free yourself from the binding of the rules and laws, there will hardly be any place for happiness in your life.

12

Maintain Equilibrium

It is health that is real wealth and not pieces of gold and silver.

—Mahatma Gandhi

'He who has health, has hope,' said Thomas Carlyle, Scottish philosopher and satirical writer. 'And he, who has hope, has everything.' Who can deny the value of health when it comes to happiness? Remember the time when you were sick or had severe pain in your body? Do you remember being happy when you were ill? A sound mind is found in a healthy body. When our body is unhealthy, our mind too is affected. If our mind is not sound, being completely happy is going to be difficult. Thousands of years ago, Buddha advised, 'To keep the body in good health is a duty...otherwise we shall not be able to keep our mind strong and clear.'

We know the importance of being healthy but only a few of us are able to manage it. We often have other priorities in life which come in the way of our desire to be healthy. We wish to be successful in life, make lots of money and achieve fame and appreciation in the world. Sometimes, we end up fulfilling these desires by sacrificing our health.

We all know the wisdom of the famous saying of Benjamin Franklin, 'Early to bed and early to rise makes a man healthy, wealthy and wise.' But we find it difficult to go to bed early because of our other engagements and then getting up early the next morning, becomes extremely difficult.

We often take our body for granted and use it as an instrument to achieve success, pleasure and make money but with disastrous results. The Dalai Lama once said, 'Man surprises me most. Because he sacrifices his health in order to make money. Then he sacrifices money to recuperate his health. And then he is so anxious about the future that he does not enjoy the present; the result being that he does not live in the present or the future; he lives as if he is never going to die, and then dies having never really lived.'

Our body and mind are not independent of each other but are two aspects of the same reality. If a sound mind is found only in a healthy body, a healthy body is also impossible without a sound mind.

- Just like every serving of food has an effect on our body, every thought has an effect on our minds.
- Just like a single bite of harmful food can ruin the health of our body, a single negative thought can ruin the peace of our mind.

Negative thoughts like hatred, envy or guilt damage our health. Our emotions are the result of our thoughts and the actions arising out of these emotions play an important role in the well-being of the body. Epictetus identified the deep connection of body, mind and soul several thousand years ago when he said, 'It takes more than just a good-looking body. You've got to have the heart and soul to go with it.'

You can find several books that teach you how to be healthy. However, following these books mechanically may give you a lean body and stout muscles but not good health, which is possible only if your mind, heart and soul are also healthy and vibrant.

Feeding Your Body

Our body is a temple for our soul. Our soul is like a little spark of God present in us. We, however, take our body for granted. We refuse to give it rest when it is sick and carry on working after taking medicines. We don't sleep properly even when our body is tired. We realise the value of health only when we lose it. Thomas Fuller, English historian, has rightly said, 'Health is not valued till sickness comes.'

The first and foremost rule for having a healthy body is to consume fresh fruits, healthy foods and drinks and avoid processed foods containing chemicals and synthetic ingredients. Avoid intoxicants, smoking or drugs that are known to be injurious to body.

A healthy body is not possible unless we balance the intake and outgo of the energies. Our diet must be in commensuration with the work we perform. It is a good habit to get up early in the morning and spend an hour walking, exercising or doing yoga and pranayama (breathing exercises). If you start your day on a positive note, you remain cheerful throughout the day.

The next important ingredient for a healthy body is adequate sleep and rest. Going to the bed at a regular time is useful for a good sleep and to start your next day afresh. It may be better to avoid stimulants such as coffee or tea just a few hours before sleep. Even eating excess of food in night can affect your sleep adversely.

Feeding Your Mind

Our thoughts are the seeds of our emotions and actions. There is a famous quote, 'Watch your thoughts, for they will become actions. Watch your actions, for they will become habits. Watch your habits, for they will forge your character. Watch your character, for it will make your destiny.'

We are often careful in avoiding foods that are bad for our health. We read the labels of packaged food to know about the ingredients and calories and then decide whether we wish to eat that food or not. Even packs of cigarettes and other tobacco products come with health warnings printed on them to help us take a judicious decision. However, no such information is available with respect to harmful thoughts, which are fed to us from all sides by the people who are interested in making profit at the cost of our mental and emotional health. We often absorb a host of thoughts without even realising their effect on our mind and body. It is important to note that the effects of the thoughts are not visible immediately but gradually they transform the mind. The negative thoughts invariably damage our body, mind and soul.

When your thoughts are not healthy, your mind loses its sacredness and vitality. It can't differentiate between right and wrong and hence, it can't guide you in the right direction.

Feeding Your Emotions

Many people believe they don't have any control over their emotions. This is not true. Our emotions are a result of the interaction of our mind and soul. On one side, we have our thoughts, that have been acquired from different sources and on the other we have our conscience that converts all thoughts into emotions. If we compare our thoughts with food, our emotions are the ingredients of the food like protein, vitamins, carbohydrates that are available in the food and get absorbed in the body gradually. For instance, the bread we eat for breakfast gets converted to sugar, carbohydrates and protein according to the requirement of the body. In the same way, our thoughts are converted to emotions like love, hatred, anger and envy by our conscience depending on the state of our mind.

A hungry man is often an angry man. If one is hungry, one's emotions are different as compared to when one is full. We have more positive thoughts after eating a nourishing, tasty meal; and we are prone to thinking more negative thoughts when we are hungry.

Our feelings and emotions are also the result of the biochemical reactions taking place in our bodies. For example, thoughts of lust are more predominant in men due to the excess amounts of testosterone in their bodies. The sexual desires of men get reduced once their testosterone levels go down. There is hardly any emotion that is not rooted in some biochemical substance in the body. Our thoughts of happiness produce health-enhancing biochemicals while sadness and depression produces harmful biochemicals and vice versa. A boost in happiness-inducing biochemicals can make you feel instantly better.

A man who desires good health must not allow negative emotions to set in his body. For example, when one is feeling angry and shouts at someone, he starts a chain of events that create more anger. The one who was at the receiving end of the anger is hurt and can hurt back in retaliation and hence hatred gets multiplied.

The release of one negative emotion triggers a chain of negative emotions in different people.

In the same way, a positive emotion sets off a series of positive activities that fulfil emotionally. For example, when we love someone and take care of someone's needs, we get the same in return and not only from that person but from others as well. That creates a happy feeling amongst everyone involved in the event. That leads to mutual exchange of positive emotions between people and the society.

Feeding Your Soul

We are not only a part of the world but we are the world. The world is incomplete without us as it is made of people like us. Everyone is connected to each other just like every single cell in the body is connected with every other cell through a network of nerves and flow of blood. If one cell of the body is in pain, the other cells of the body can't live peacefully.

We need to help others in order to make ourselves happy and create a better world. When we are only taking from the world and not giving anything in return, we are creating an imbalance in our spiritual energies. If we develop the habit of giving back to the world as much as we are taking from it, we feed our souls and lead a more vibrant life.

Take Care of Your Complete Being

It is important to integrate our body, mind, heart and soul to achieve a perfect equilibrium in our life. When they are in tune with each other like good friends and have an understanding with each other, we develop integrity within and without. This integrity provides a seamless flow of all energies that connects us strongly with the world. We achieve happiness. As Mahatma Gandhi said, 'Happiness is when what you think, what you say, and what you do are in harmony.'

A happy person maintains equilibrium between his body, mind, heart and soul by taking care of his complete self. He knows that they are all connected with each other and they all complement each other.

13

Manage Your Love

To love is to place our happiness in the happiness of another.
—G Wilhelm Leibniz, German philosopher

It is difficult to imagine happiness without love. Oliver Wendell Homes, American jurist, rightly said, 'Love is the master key that opens the gate of happiness.' Love and happiness are so intricately connected with each other that they appear to be one. When we have love in our hearts, we relate at a much deeper level with other people and we get loved by them. When we love someone, we care for their happiness more than our own happiness.

Love is the surge of positive and ecstatic feeling towards our beloved. When we are in love, we view the person as perfect and see only the good things of that person. When someone points out to us any negative qualities about our beloved, we don't like it and defend her or him as if the accusation was made against our own selves. We wish to make our loved ones as happy as possible because when our loved ones are happy, we feel twice as happy. This poem *Which Loved Best?* by Joy Allison beautifully narrates what true love is.

'I love you, Mother,' said little John;
Then, forgetting his work, his cap went on,
And he was off to the garden-swing,
Leaving his mother the wood to bring.

'I love you, Mother,' said rosy Nell;
'I love you better than tongue can tell';
Then she teased and pouted full half the day,
Till her mother rejoiced when she went to play.

'I love you, Mother,' said little Fan;
'Today I'll help you all I can;
How glad I am that school doesn't keep!'
So she rocked the baby till it fell asleep.

Then, stepping softly, she took the broom,
And swept the floor and dusted the room;
Busy and happy all day was she,
Helpful and cheerful as child could be.

'I love you, Mother,' again they said—
Three little children going to bed,
How do you think that Mother guessed
Which of them really loved her best?

Love is manifested through our actions where involuntarily we reach out to help those whom we love.

When you love your mother, helping her becomes a joy in itself and needs no appreciation or reward.

Different Dimensions of Love

Love is one of the most misunderstood and misused terms in the modern world. People claim to love their cars, mobile phones, country and even their language. Often like gets misunderstood as love. Even lust, passion and sex are increasingly confused with love. Making love is now synonymous with having sex. Figure 1 illustrates the three dimensions of love.

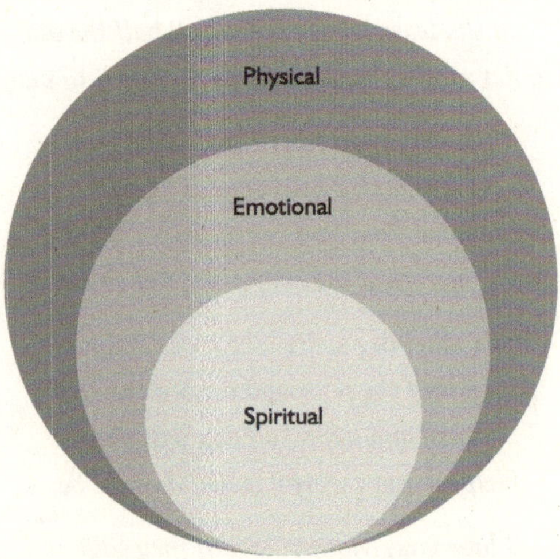

Figure 1: Three Dimensions of Love

Physical Love

The common, spontaneous and powerful form of love is physical. This is the natural form of love that is found in all species and is required for procreation. It is the desire for pleasure that drives physical love. The attraction between opposite sexes is so powerful that it shadows all other forms of love. A man is attracted towards beautiful women. The occurrence of this attraction is natural because nature warrants such type of attraction for procreation. Without such attractions the human race would have become extinct long ago.

Physical love is also often called lust. People commanded by the power of lust are willing to give anything to get the object of their desire for the fulfilment of their physical needs. If the other person does not reciprocate, they become miserable. Some people in their desperation may even go to the extent of hurting themselves or their beloved.

However, lust loses its grip over the person once it is quenched. Lust alone can't bind a couple to each other for long. Hence, relationships based on lust do not last as sex becomes routine and boring very soon. The couple loses interest in each other after they have explored each other fully. They start craving for a different experience. They often fall for extra-marital relationships or part ways for a new partner.

Emotional Love

Emotional love comes from our heart in the form of emotions and feelings. We feel love for our children, our parents, our beloved as also for our pets. Once we develop a loving relationship with someone or something, we also develop reasons for our feelings.

In the poem, the little girl Fan was driven to action due to her feeling for her mother. In the movie *Titanic*, the hero gives his life up for the heroine because he was driven by his emotion of love for her. Emotional love is so powerful that people fall in love under its attraction. Emotional love binds people by an unseen thread that keeps the family and the society together.

Spiritual Love

The deepest form of love is difficult to explain as it comes from the core of human beings. It is called spiritual love which is all-encompassing and eternal. Some people also call it unconditional love because it remains even after all other forms of love have dissipated. If you are spiritual, you feel connected with everyone by a spiritual bond. Your beloved becomes a part of you and your soul expands to encompass her soul. You always try to make others happy even if it means sacrificing your own happiness.

Spiritual love is possible only when the body, mind and heart of the person are in sync with the soul, and your soul gets connected with every soul of the universe. The flow of spiritual love is natural and effortless once you overcome personal desires and self-gratification. In fact, not to love another person would need effort from a spiritual person.

Creating Love in Your Heart

Love is one of the most important ingredients for happiness. However, many people don't feel love for others in their heart and fail to win love from others. What can they do to create love in their heart or be loved by others?

It is possible to create love in your life through loving actions.

Just like feelings drive action, we can use action to transform our feelings. If you perform actions akin to those in love, your actions generate similar feelings. You can create love in your heart by doing things as if you are in love. The best example is perhaps with a pet. When we bring up our pet like a child, we gradually start loving it like a child.

One effective way to create love in your heart is to focus on the positives of the person whom you wish to love. Since every person has a good and a not-so-good side, you can find some lovable qualities in every person. You must praise him whenever he does something good, while avoid criticising him for his mistakes. Once you start seeing the positive side of a person, you will feel his positive image growing and his negative image diminishing in your mind. Your feelings would soon follow your actions and you would start liking and eventually loving the person.

Nurture Love with Action

Love is like a living being with a body and a soul. The soul of love is emotion while the body of love is action. Just like body and soul are integrated, emotions and actions too are integrated. You do some loving actions naturally when you feel love for a person. But, if the actions are missing, even though the feelings might be there, love can't survive for long.

You can even create love in the heart of unknown people by performing actions similar to those which one does for his beloved. You can thus plant the seed of love in the heart of other people and develop love in them. This would soon fructify and make your life full of love.

Manage Your Love to Avoid Suffering

While love is the source of happiness, it may also become a source of pain. Ambrose Gwinnett Bierce, an American satirist, writer and journalist defined romantic love as following:

> Love: A temporary insanity curable by marriage or by removal of the patient from the influences under which he incurred the disorder. This disease is prevalent only among civilised races living under artificial conditions; barbarous nations breathing pure air and eating simple food enjoy immunity from its ravages. It is sometimes fatal, but more frequently to the physician than to the patient.

The famous poet Mirza Ghalib also said, 'Understand that this love is not easy. It is a river of fire and you have to go drowning.'

When you love, you also suffer the pain of detachment from your beloved and share her pains and miseries. If your love is not reciprocated or your beloved loves someone else, your pain is worse than being burnt in fire. Hence, love should not be treated as panacea for all happiness and excessive love or love at the wrong place or for wrong people can become a source of tremendous pain and misery.

Many people when in love lose their balance of life and end up making their lives miserable.

- Excessive love for physical pleasure is responsible for most of the world's crime, including rape, murder and robbery.
- Excessive love for one's own country is responsible for ultra-nationalism which often leads to war between nations.
- The love for God often leads to animosity and wars between followers of different religions, and terrorism.
- Spiritual love sometimes becomes a source of pain because when you love everyone, you also feel the pain of everyone. The more you expand your soul, the higher becomes your pain.

While it is important in life to love, it is even more important to not be consumed by love.

Saints and wise men have, therefore, advised people to shun attachment and practice detachment.

A proper balance of love and detachment is the best recipe for happiness.

14

Contentment Brings Happiness

Be thankful for what you have; you'll end up having more. If you concentrate on what you don't have, you will never, ever have enough.

—Oprah Winfrey

It is almost impossible to be happy unless you are satisfied and content with what you have. The Merriam Webster even defines Happiness as 'a state of well-being and contentment.' Yet, how many of us are content with our lives? Most people are unhappy since they are always striving for more. There are ample studies to demonstrate that the happiness levels in people do not change much with an increase in wealth or power.

When we get a promotion or a raise in salary, we feel happy for some time. However, very soon we get used to the higher salary as we increase our expenses in the same proportion. Once you get a promotion or a better-paying job, you shift to a bigger house, buy a more expensive car, bigger television sets and a more expensive mobile phone. You increase your expenses quite fast and even buy couple of things on credit card. Once your expenses have increased more than what your income can sustain, you are back to leading a miserable life again. Often people take loans to buy things they may not really need and then pay a large amount of monthly instalment to pay off that loan and that reduces their take-home salary even after the pay hike.

A few years ago, one of my friends wanted to purchase a flat in Delhi. He was earlier working in a public sector company and getting a nominal salary. Then, he purchased a flat in the suburbs for just Rs 1.5 million ($20,000). After a few years, he got a job overseas and his salary multiplied by more than ten times in the next ten years. So he planned to buy a flat in a posh locality of Delhi and his budget was then Rs 15 million. However, when he started looking for a flat in the area of his choice, he found that nothing was available for less than Rs 25 million. Exasperated he told me resignedly, 'Awdhesh, I don't know why our income is always so inadequate when it comes to buying a property.' I told him that the problem lies in our rising expectations. Had he got Rs 25 million, he would have wanted to purchase an even more expensive flat, in a pricier locality and that would have cost Rs 50 million and again he would have felt inadequate. I told him that within his budget, there are hundreds of good options available, but he would probably not like them simply because of his higher expectations.

If we can't enjoy our increased salary or the promotions, the fault lies with us. In my own case, I have learnt to be content within my income. In the last ten years, my salary has gone up almost four times. However, I have increased my expenses to only less than twice, despite the inflation. I continue to own the same car that I purchased a decade ago and since it is running perfectly fine even now, I don't see much point in changing it. I still go to similar types of restaurants for dining and wear similar brands of clothes as earlier. The result is that not only do I find my salary sufficient, but I am also able to save almost 40 per cent of my salary. My savings have given me so much of bank balance that I feel much more secure and rich now. I have, however, found that many of my colleagues are still complaining about low salaries and increase in the expenses because they have increased their expenses much more than the rise in salary. I take lesson from Pablo Picasso who once said, 'I'd like to live as a poor man with lots of money.'

If you are thinking that I have made sacrifice of my joy in the process, you can't be more wrong. The fact is that this simple life has given me much more joy. There is nothing that I desire and I don't have. It is because I have worked on reducing my desires and increasing my contentment.

The Magic of Contentment

If you are forced to give up something that you love and desire, you become frustrated and unhappy. However, if you have to give up something that you didn't like in the first place, you feel relieved.

We often spend money dining in expensive restaurants or in five-star hotels where the food is great, ambience is pleasant and the service is good. You might need to shell out Rs 5000 each time you dine in a luxury hotel. So if you are a family of four, you may end up spending around Rs 20,000 on just the dining and the transport. You can get similar quality of food in a lesser luxurious environment, but in a decent hotel at just Rs 500 per head. If you prepare the same dishes at your home, it may cost you just Rs 500 for the entire family.

However, money is not the only thing that you pay when dining in a five-star hotel. You may also end up consuming two or three times more calories while dining out. You have to then torture your body for a couple of hours more—jogging, walking or exercising—to burn those extra calories and maintain your weight. If you avoid the post-dining-out torture, you may gain weight every time you dine out and gradually you will become obese, unhealthy and unattractive. You also spend a lot more time in dining out since you have to travel from your home to the hotel and wait for the food to be served. While the joy of tasty food lasts on your tongue only for few minutes, its effect on your pocket and your body stays longer.

Hence, by keeping your food habits simple, you not only save money and time but also keep better health. The money saved would save time because you will not need to work extra hours to earn the additional money needed for such expenses. You can afford to choose a lesser-paying but more interesting job if you can manage to keep your expenses in check. Thus, you can increase your happiness at your workplace and home by simplifying your habits.

Dining out is still only a minor part of your expenditures. An expensive car may set you back by huge sums of money and reduce your take-home income substantially after adjusting the monthly instalments. Today, even the most ordinary car comes fitted with air conditioners and all the features, which till a few years back were provided only in the luxury cars. You can buy a good car even for Rs 70,000 or pay a crore to buy a Ferrari or Lamborghini. The comfort may vary only a little but the price difference is enormous.

Most people buy expensive cars only to impress others because they may have no other personal quality of their own to earn attention and respect from others. Why not buy an average car and save the excess money to provide security for the future? What holds good for a car also holds good for a house where there is virtually no upper limit to the pricing. Why not live in a small and decent house that can give you almost as much comfort as living in a mansion? John Stuart Mill, British philosopher and political economist, had rightly said, 'I have learned to seek my happiness by limiting my desires, rather than in attempting to satisfy them.'

In reality, our needs are very few. Our basic needs of food, water, clothing and shelter can be fulfilled by only a small amount of money. However, there is no limit to our greed and megalomania.

Mahatma Gandhi once said, 'The world has enough for everyone's need, but not enough for everyone's greed.'

I will go a step further and say, 'The world has enough for everyone's need, but not enough to satisfy even one person's greed.'

I believe human greed is infinite and can't be satisfied even with the entire wealth of the world. It is always better to work on the demand side (desire) than on the supply side (income) to lead a contented life.

Big businesses, operating worldwide, not only create goods but also create needs. When people are unhappy with their present state, they buy more goods and services to become happy. Just like we don't want to go to a doctor when we are healthy, a contented man would never be tempted to buy new things to make himself happy. A doctor becomes richer when more people fall sick. Similarly, the more unhappy people are in the society, the easier it is for the businesses to sell them their products and services with the lure of happiness.

A clever businessman convinces you that your life is miserable because you don't have a big car, or you don't have the latest mobile phone or you don't live in a big house filled with numerous luxuries.

- How can you be happy unless you eat the food that they make in their kitchen with their expert chefs?
- How can you enjoy life until you visit the exotic locations that they want you to see?

They hire top models and celebrities to seed these messages in your subconscious mind and use all channels of communication such as television, internet and newspapers to deliver the message to you. There is no way you can escape them. You can understand their game plan and avoid falling into their trap only when you are happy and satisfied with your life. When you are unhappy, you are in their clutches just like a sick man is in the clutches of doctors. Once you are caught in the trap of money-buys-happiness, it will be very tough for you to free yourself. Your life will become even more miserable if you heed their advice and spend your hard-earned money on their products. You may soon be addicted to buying momentary happiness from money, and that will ensure you are always buying their goods and services.

If you know what you want and discover true happiness in what you have, you do not need to buy expensive things to prove to the world that you are happy. Thousands of years ago, Lao Tzu said,

Because one believes in oneself,
one doesn't try to convince others.
Because one is content with oneself,
one doesn't need others' approval.
Because one accepts oneself,
the whole world accepts him or her.

Once you learn to live within your means and be content with what you are and what you have, you are happy without any effort.

15

No Happiness Without Freedom

We hold these truths to be self-evident: that all men are created equal; that they are endowed by their Creator with certain unalienable rights; that among these are life, liberty and the pursuit of happiness.

—Thomas Jefferson

It is difficult to enjoy happiness without freedom. Even if you are a king and live in a palace made of gold with all luxuries at your disposal, you can't be happy if you don't have free will to exercise. Sant Tulsidas, the famous poet and author of the epic *Ramacharitamanas* wisely said, 'A man who is dependent on others can't enjoy happiness even in his dreams.'

There are different types of freedom. They are:

- Freedom to experiment

- Freedom to choose jobs
- Freedom to do your job in your own way
- Freedom to choose spouse
- Freedom at home

However, we hardly enjoy freedom in this world. We feel enslaved by our family, organisation, country and the society. We often don't exercise our freedom even when it is granted to us by the laws of the land. George Bernard Shaw explained, 'Liberty means responsibility. That is why most men dread it.'

People are reluctant to exercise their freedom in spite of having earned it. Even when people reach the top of the bureaucratic or managerial ladder, and possess power to take important decisions, they avoid it. If they can't avoid taking the decision, they often want someone else to take the responsibility. Most of them prefer to pass the buck onto their bosses. If they can't pass the buck upwards, they pass it downwards. They keep consulting others for decision-making, so that if the decision fails, they can easily blame someone else for the ensuing mishaps. Most people prefer taking the safest decision so that if it fails, it causes them minimum inconvenience. However, with such safe approach in life, we can hardly enjoy life. This poem 'A Very Cautious Man' states this truth interestingly.

There was a very cautious man,
Who never romped and played,
He never smoked, He never drank,
Nor ever kissed a maid.

And when he up and passed away,
His insurance was denied.
For since he hadn't ever lived,
They claimed he never died.

Mahatma Gandhi said, 'Freedom is not worth having if it does not imply the freedom to err.' If people don't want to use their freedom, it is because they fear that their judgments may not be right and they may be later blamed for the ensuing failures. In order to avoid the pain of failure, they avoid taking decisions itself and forgo all their freedom.

We must remember that pain is just the other side of joy. If you avoid all possibilities to pain, you also block all avenues of happiness. It is like writing an examination. If you want to be absolutely sure that you don't fail, you don't write the examination. However, by doing so, you also block all your chances of success.

The Cycle of Freedom and Bondage

There are three stages of every matter. Physicists define these three stages as solid, liquid and gas. In the solid state, all the molecules of the material are fixed in their position. They have no freedom to move. In the liquid state, the molecules have the freedom to move within the volume of liquid. In the gaseous state, there is no restriction on movement whatsoever. An oxygen molecule can move from one part to any other part of the world unhindered.

Nature needs all the three states of matter to exist.

A solid matter gets converted to liquid if given sufficient energy. A liquid substance is transformed to gas if given even more energy. Similarly, when the energy is dissipated, matter cools down and gas is liquefied and then solidified. For example, water is usually found on earth in liquid form. It is evaporated by the heat of the sun and becomes a gaseous cloud in sky. Then, it rains and gives nourishment to Mother Earth. However, some rain falls on glaciers and mountains and becomes solid ice. Then, this solid form of water becomes liquid gradually and provides water to the rivers round the year. This water flows back to the sea from where it again gets evaporated. Thus, this cycle of nature continues forever for the nourishment of all species and living things on earth.

We can see similar things happening in the world of social relationships as well. When we are young and don't have much resources, we are dependent upon our parents for all our needs. We are in the bondage of relationships which restricts our freedom. However, as we grow up and have sufficient resources, we wish to leave the bondage of parental home and want to become free to live a life of our own choosing.

All teenagers enjoy freedom but they get bored of it. They want to be in relationships that will provide them security and stability. They seek marriage and employment, which on one side bind them and on the other side give them freedom from the relationship of their parents. As soon as they get freedom from one relationship (parental), they get into another relationship (marriage) and soon forgo their freedom—yet again. The cycle of freedom and bondage thus continues throughout our lives. We live in an interdependent world where there is no possibility of absolute freedom. We can't survive alone in this world.

Happiness requires love, being in a relationship, compassion, intimacy as well as freedom. Every relationship binds you with others, thereby reducing your freedom to some extent. There is no possibility of absolute freedom for man. However, it is possible to increase our freedom to maximise our happiness.

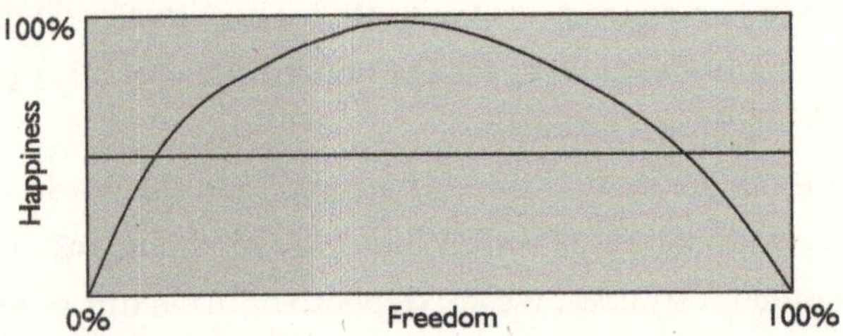

Figure 1: Schematic Diagram of Freedom and Happiness

Figure 1 illustrates the relationship between freedom and happiness. Too much of freedom is as much responsible for unhappiness as too little freedom. In order to enjoy maximum happiness, we must have a balance of freedom and a binding relationship.

Freedom in an Interdependent World

We may feel free when we aren't dependent on anyone for doing what we wish to do in our lives. When our freedom is restricted for long, we become desperate to be free.

Sometimes we get so desperate to break free that we feel that any alternative is better than the existing one. However, most of the time, we find that by escaping from the present without knowing where to go, we make our lives more miserable. Eric Hoffer, the American moral and social philosopher has said, 'We feel free when we escape—even if it be but from the frying pan into the fire.'

I have a few friends who are so frustrated of bearing their responsibilities—of their job and family—that they dream of retiring early and enjoying their post-retirement life in some countryside or in some peaceful hill station. They find their home and office atmosphere quite suffocating as they feel weighed down with duties and responsibilities.

I have, however, discovered freedom at home amidst all the relationships and humdrum of life. Often, I take leave for weeks or even months from the job and stay at home. I read, write, watch movies and sometimes visit commendable places with family. Instead of going in and staying in a tourist destination, I prefer to stay at home in familiar surroundings and with all amenities. Staying at a hotel, resort or camp is not only expensive but also quite boring after sometime because you start to feel starved emotionally due to the lack of connection with your friends and other members of the family. It is possible to make your home the most peaceful place where everyone enjoys freedom and company of each other.

We love being in relationships with other people if we are in a commanding position. However, when we have to obey others, we seek freedom. If you align your desires with the desires of others, there wouldn't be a need for freedom.

The quest for freedom in the real world is like living in a room with many windows. You can connect with the outside atmosphere whenever you want to, by opening the windows and when you seek privacy or solitude, you can close them.

When you are in harmony with others, life becomes a celebration because you can bring happiness to the lives of numerous people associated with you. The interdependence does not prick you as you love being with people and wish to make their lives better. When you give joy to others, you get back much more joy in your life.

16

Manage Your Time

The key is not to prioritise what's on your schedule, but to schedule your priorities.

—Stephen Covey, American educator and author

Albert Einstein was once asked to explain the concept of relativity. He replied, 'Put your hand on a hot stove for a minute, and it seems like an hour. Sit with a pretty girl for an hour, and it seems like a minute. That's relativity.'

We know that time does not flow evenly for everyone all the time. When we are happy, time 'flows' so fast that we don't even come to realise that several hours and even days have passed. However, when we are suffering, time seems to be never ending. When you are at a traffic signal waiting for it to become green and you are getting late for an important meeting, every single second seems like eternity.

We all have the same amount of time in a day—twenty-four hours. However, there are some people who have all the time in the world, while there are many who are always running short of time. I once worked with a colleague, who used to be so busy in his work that he would frequently say, 'I have no time to breathe.' He hardly could take out time to sip a coffee with a friend who may be visiting him after several years. Being busy, however, did not make him more efficient and productive. He was soon replaced by another officer who had ample time not only to breathe but also to complete all the chores at hand. Jim Rohn, an American entrepreneur, author and motivational speaker, once said, 'Don't mistake movement for achievement. It's easy to get faked out by being busy. The question is: Busy doing what?'

You must have come across people who are working all the time yet have failed to produce results. This 'busyness-syndrome' starts at an early age. During school days, you can find many students who study all the time but still never achieve good results in the examinations. Yet there are a few others who produce great results almost effortlessly. During school, your examination results reflect your performance and not the number of hours you spent studying. The relationship between working hours and performance is not linear. Your performance starts deteriorating if you spend too less time or spend too much time on your job.

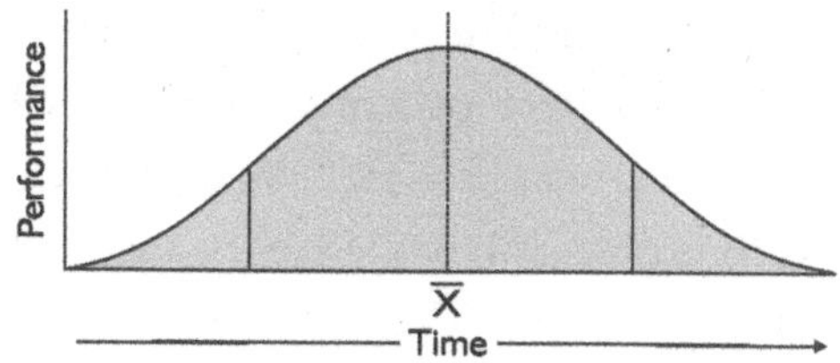

Figure 1: Time-Performance Relationship

Figure 1 shows the relationship between time and performance. When you don't work at all, your performance is poor. It starts improving as you devote more hours to your job. However, it peaks at a certain point beyond which, if you continue spending more time on work, it starts deteriorating. Our wisdom lies in identifying this point of inflection when our efficiency is the best.

We must know when to stop exerting to maintain the optimum level of productivity. A man who has no time for enjoyment is no better than a person who has no ability to enjoy.

(1) Unimportant & Interesting	(2) Important & Uninteresting
(3) Unimportant & Uninteresting	(4) Important & Interesting

Figure 2: Classification of Assignments

Figure 2 is a schematic diagram of the types of works and our attitude towards the related works. There are some jobs which are quite unpleasant like putting-your-hand-in-stove, while there are some other very interesting jobs like talking-to-a-beautiful-girl. We usually like to do the work which is pleasant, while we try and avoid what is unpleasant.

We have the tendency to choose the interesting work first. Time flies when we are doing an interesting job. We are so immersed in the pleasure of the task that we don't want to come out of it. We often waste too much time doing interesting things, so much so, that we are left with little time to do important jobs, which may be uninteresting.

Once we have completed the pleasant work, we are left only with unpleasant tasks. We don't wish to think about those chores after coming out of the stupor of our beautiful moments that we spent doing interesting jobs. The result is that such unpleasant tasks are postponed and sometimes never get done.

You don't get many interesting things to do in your daily life. Even the most pleasant task gradually becomes boring and unpleasant. With passage of time, more and more activities are added to the list of unpleasant things and the list of pleasant tasks becomes smaller. Having nothing interesting to do, we have no alternative but to complete the unpleasant tasks that have been piling up on our table for a long time. Now the time seems to have stopped as we suffer the torture of doing such unpleasant tasks all together.

It would be much better to delegate the unimportant and the less important work to your subordinates even if it is interesting so that you are free to do the important work, whether interesting or not. Such an action would empower your junior team members and provide them the training to take up more important work later on. Such an action would also give you more time to do important work, plan for the future and complete your work within the given time frame.

Importance or Pleasure

Happy people choose work according to its importance rather than on the basis of how interesting or pleasurable the task is. If you take up the important but uninteresting work first, you will be more focused on the work due to its importance even if it is uninteresting. You must take up such work when you are in your best mood and full of energy, for example, early in the morning or in the first hour of the office.

The most intriguing thing about choosing an important but less interesting job is that it challenges you. The duller the job, the more challenging it is since not many people are willing to take up such tasks. However, once you get into this challenging job, the same job gradually becomes very interesting and satisfying. Mihaly Csikszentmihalyi, a Hungrian-American psychologist and author, explains in his book *Flow: The Psychology of Optimal Experience*, 'Most enjoyable activities are not natural; they demand an effort that initially one is reluctant to make. But once the interaction starts to provide feedback to the person's skills, it usually begins to be intrinsically rewarding.'

Once you successfully complete important but uninteresting work with your best state of mind, you may find an erstwhile interesting work even more interesting just like cold water feels even cooler if you dip your hand in it just after dipping it in hot water. Also, it is fascinating to note that when you are anticipating a pleasant work ahead, even the painful work appears more tolerable in anticipation of interesting work that will follow, just like a long journey that becomes pleasurable, if the destination is very beautiful.

When you complete your unpleasant work first, you have no difficulty in completing the pleasant work thereafter.

In our personal life also, there are many important tasks that are not pleasant. For example, every person knows the importance of fitness in leading a healthy and happy life. One easy way to keep fit is to do a morning walk or workout regularly. These activities are hardly pleasant in the beginning. However, if you follow the routine of doing morning walk and exercise, you gradually train your mind to take the important-but-unpleasant task first and let other interesting activities of the day wait till your difficult but important job is over. If you follow this regime, you will find that even the other daily activities throughout the day become more enjoyable.

Who can make you unhappy, if you have developed the ability to enjoy even difficult and uninteresting jobs?

Sometimes we waste time because we wish to do pleasant-but-unimportant work. If we find the work of our subordinates more interesting, we want to do that job more than our own. As we start from junior positions and gradually rise to higher levels in an organisation, we, by the virtue of experience, can often do such jobs better than our subordinates, who may lack experience and expertise. It is common to come across some bosses who are more interested in doing the jobs of their subordinates and try to micro-manage them instead of focusing on their own work, which is more important but may not be as interesting. The result is that their juniors often lose morale because the boss is always trying to improve their work and they gradually let their boss do everything which otherwise is their task. Hence, they have lots of free time while boss is slogging all day doing the work not only his own but also of his subordinates. The original work of the boss is thus rarely completed on time.

Hence, the work which can be done by your subordinates should be delegated, even if you like doing the work yourself. You must rather focus only on those tasks that can be done by you alone. If you still have some time left, focus on future planning and improving the efficiency of the organisation.

It is important to understand that lack of time is no less a source of unhappiness than lack of money. The more time you can save for yourself, the more time you will have to enjoy life and do what you love to do. A man, who is rich in time, is no less wealthy than a man who is rich in money.

Transmutation of Pleasure and Pain

You must have experienced in your life how sometimes even the most interesting activity gradually loses its pleasure quotient and becomes a pain. When we find something pleasant, we keep on doing it till we are tired or bored of it. The Gita warns us against such sensual pleasures that we get from our nature of passion (Rajas), 'the pleasures which arise from the contact of the senses with their objects; which first look like nectar but in the end like poison.' (*Gita 18:38*)

The good news is that just like pleasure can become pain with repeated use, we can also transform painful activities into pleasant ones with practice. Most of us don't know this great truth because we are always trying to avoid the painful activities right from the very beginning. We never reach the other side of the pain that is pleasure. The pleasure that comes from enjoying activities, which were painful in the beginning, is indeed true joy. Lord Krishna called such pleasures 'Sattvik' (pleasure of truth). It is defined as: 'Pleasure which is enjoyed by repeated practice and which puts an end to the pain; which in its inception looks like poison but in the end is like nectar; which is born of serene realisation of the true nature of self.' (*Gita 18:36-37*)

Let us recall some activities which we did not like in the beginning but later they became our passion.

For example, children rarely like to read or go to school. Most children simply want to play and enjoy good food. However, if they keep studying, they gradually develop interest in learning and start loving it. Thereafter, nothing gives the same child more pleasure than reading books and acquiring knowledge.

The famous management guru Peter Drucker said, 'Executives are not paid for doing things they like to do. They are paid for getting the right things done—most of all in their specific task, the making of effective decisions.' He adds, 'There is no inherent reason why medicines should taste horrible, but effective ones usually do. Similarly, there is no inherent reason why decisions should be distasteful—but most effective ones are.'

Once you learn to bite the bullet by taking tough decisions, you will surprisingly develop a liking for taking such decisions, which may appear quite unpleasant in the beginning but produce wonderful results for the organisation and develop your skills.

A good doctor should not avoid performing surgery or prescribing a bitter pill if it is in the interest of the patient. Similarly, a wise person must not avoid taking unpleasant and difficult decisions, if they are in the interest of the people and the organisation.

Creating Wealth of Time

If we develop the habit of focusing our attention on doing the right things first, whether they are pleasant or unpleasant, we soon develop the skill of finishing our job quickly and create a surplus of time to enjoy and plan for the future. When we take a bitter pill, we ensure quick recovery from illness so that we can finish the job with renewed enthusiasm. Mihaly Csikszentmihalyi, the author of *Flow: The Psychology of Optimal Experience* said this beautifully:

> Contrary to what we usually believe, moments like these, the best moments in our lives, are not the passive, receptive, relaxing times—although such experiences can also be enjoyable, if we have worked hard to attain them. The best moments usually occur when a person's body or mind is stretched to its limits in a voluntary effort to accomplish something difficult and worthwhile. Optimal experience is thus something that we make happen. For a child, it could be placing with trembling fingers the last block on a tower she has built, higher than any she has built so far; for a swimmer, it could be trying to beat his own record; for a violinist, mastering an intricate musical passage. For each person there are thousands of opportunities, challenges to expand ourselves.

No task can remain painful to a man who has mastered his pain and converted it to a pleasure. Such a person enjoys doing everything. Hence, his life is filled with joy.

17

Anger Destroys Happiness

There are two things a person should never be angry at, what they can help, and what they cannot.

—Plato

Anger is an extreme emotional state of mind that gets triggered automatically when we are faced with undesirable or unexpected situations. When you are angry, your body's muscles tense up. Inside the brain, a set of neurotransmitter chemicals known as catecholamine get released that cause a burst of energy lasting up to several minutes. At the same time, the heartbeat increases, the blood pressure rises, and so does the rate of breathing. Your face may get flushed due to the increased blood flow. In quick succession, additional brain neurotransmitters and hormones, adrenaline and noradrenaline are released, that trigger a lasting state of arousal. This extra energy prepares us to fight the danger ahead.

Our emotions overtake our reasoning mind when we are angry. Often we do something or say something that harms not only others but ourselves as well. We may repent our outbursts of anger later on but the scar created due to the harsh words, spoken in the fit of anger, does not get healed even in a lifetime. Sometimes, an episode of small anger may trigger a fight with some unknown people leading to unfortunate consequences like murder. It is not uncommon to hear incidences of road rage in big cities, when extreme anger on small issues like not giving a right to pass, or even honking can lead to a fight in which people are grievously injured or even killed.

Anger may be nature's mechanism for the survival of species, but we can control anger by proper practice and by developing deep understanding.

> A big, tough samurai once went to see a little monk. He barked, in a voice accustomed to instant obedience: 'Teach me about heaven and hell!'
>
> The monk looked up at the mighty warrior and replied with utter disdain: 'Teach you about heaven and hell? I can't teach you about anything. You're dumb. You're dirty. You're a disgrace, an embarrassment to the samurai class. Get out of my sight. I can't stand you.'
>
> The samurai got furious. He shook, red in the face, speechless with rage. He pulled out his sword, and prepared to slay the monk.
>
> Looking straight into the samurai's eyes, the monk said softly, 'That's hell.'

The samurai froze, realising the compassion of the monk who had risked his life to show him hell! He put down his sword and fell to his knees, filled with gratitude.

The monk said softly, 'And that's heaven.'

We create our own hell or heaven by giving vent to anger or by mastering it. If you are angry, the world seems like hell. However, when you are peaceful, the same world becomes heaven.

Reasons to be Angry

If you consider anger natural, you can always find numerous reasons to justify your anger.

- You may get angry because your boss does not listen to you.
- You may get angry because the leaders of your country are corrupt.
- You may be angry because the world has been unjust to you and to other people like you.
- Children are angry when their parents shout at them.
- Parents are angry when their children don't study but waste their time in playing, gossiping or being hyperactive on social media.

There are millions of reasons to be angry and people are often in a foul mood due to anger. Aristotle said wisely, 'Anybody can become angry, that is easy. But to be angry with the right person and to the right degree and at the right time and for the right purpose, and in the right way—that is not within everybody's power and is not easy.'

People get angry when others don't work according to what they think is right. Even in your family, when your spouse and children do not listen to you and all your wishes are not followed, you can end up losing your temper. We resent our subordinates when they don't follow our instructions and keep doing things in their own way. We are upset when our bosses tell us to do something, which we think is not right.

It is natural to feel angry once in a while, but it becomes a serious problem when you are getting angry regularly even in routine situations at home or in the office. When the anger becomes frequent and flares up at the slightest provocation, it is an indication that all is not well in your life. Frequent and uncontrolled anger is a symptom of a fragile state of mind, which gets manifested at the slightest unfavourable situation.

Once our anger has settled down and our rational mind is back in action, we realise the damage we have done to ourselves and to other people in the fit of rage. Even the most sagacious man can become a beast when he loses his temper. But remember that just like a house burnt by fire can't be brought back even after the fire is dowsed, no amount of repentance can restore the damage caused by your lost temper. Your unhappiness and frustration will only mount with every outbreak of anger and you stand the risk of being discarded by your friends and relatives to whom you caused emotional distress in your angry moments.

Can You Prevent Anger?

Anger puts us in unexpected situations. Anger comes naturally to those of us who are unprepared for the future. For example, when you have an important meeting to attend or a job interview and you get stuck in a traffic jam, your first reaction is of getting angry. You start cursing the traffic light, the traffic inspector, the government and the unruly public for the jam. You may even get angry at your own self for starting late or at your relative who dropped at your place at the last moment causing the delay. However, as soon as you reach office, you forget all about the traffic jam that aroused anger in you. If you are not punished for coming late, you forget the incident without learning any lessons from it.

However, if you remember your anger and the unhappiness it caused to you, you can avoid getting into such a situation in future. You can develop the habit to start from home a few minutes early, particularly before important meetings. This habit will provide you with some extra time to take care of the delays, if any. If you plan a few minutes extra for the possible traffic jam, you can eliminate the flaring up of anger almost completely. Once in a while, if something totally unexpected happens, you can inform your boss and you will be pardoned for arriving late due to your past record of punctuality.

In the same way, we get angry at some type of people. If we can avoid these people to the best possible extent, our instances of getting angry will come down.

If you are getting angry at your boss who frequently finds fault with your work, you can avoid that by doing your job better and leaving little room for fault finding.

We can prevent anger to a very large extent by anticipating its causes and planning in advance. A person who gets angry frequently is a person who has not planned well enough to tackle any unexpected situations from cropping up. The better your planning is, lesser the chances of you having to face any unexpected situations and lesser becomes the chance of your getting angry.

Building Up Anger Inside

We can understand anger by using the analogy of a pressure cooker. Pressure cookers are quite popular around the world for cooking efficiently. They work on the mechanism where the steam is trapped inside by blocking its exit by a 'whistle'. When the steam is trapped inside the cooker, pressure starts building up. When the pressure inside increases beyond a point, the whistle gets lifted with the steam and in the process the pressure is released with a shrieking sound made by the whistle.

Like a pressure cooker, our mind also can't remain cool if pressure gets built up inside it due to frequent adverse situations. Every adverse situation builds some pressure in our mind. This mental pressure gives rise to negative emotions. When you constantly live in a state of high arousal, even the slightest provocation may lead to lifting of the whistle and loss of temper.

The first step to contain anger is to contain the heat itself that is generated inside our minds due to adverse situations. If you live life with few adversaries and more friends, chances of agitation in your mind are lesser. This can be done by spending more time with people whom you like and avoiding the company of unknown or hostile people.

People are like a mathematical puzzle. If you don't know them, they seem difficult. However, once you understand them, they are a game. If you understand a person completely, you can deal with him as simply as you deal with yourself. If you know the nature of fire, you will not burn your fingers in it. Instead, you would use it for cooking your food.

However, when you are dealing with a large number of unknown people, your mind has to work overtime because it is under pressure to try and figure them out properly. This creates mental fatigue from excessive use of your thought processes.

If you understand the personalities of most people who are close to you, you take care of almost all the unexpected situations that could flare up anger. Hence, even when you have to occasionally deal with some difficult people or situations, you have a store of peaceful energy inside you that will help deal with them without inducing fatigue. It is like having a large amount of water in store to douse the fire that has expectedly flared up at your place.

The whistle of the pressure cooker won't blow up with the first flare of energy. Similarly, it takes time to accumulate pressure inside us and get blown up in anger.

Safe Release of Anger

Buddha once said, 'Holding on to anger is like grasping a hot coal with the intent of throwing it at someone else; you are the one who gets burned.' We must find a safe release of the anger before it bursts unexpectedly and causes huge loss to ourselves and others.

One effective way to release anger is to discuss it with someone who is peaceful and trustworthy. When you share your thoughts with trusted people, your anger loses most of its steam. However, the lasting solution of anger can be found only when you can avoid its creation itself. One of the effective ways to do that is to take responsibility of being angry and understand that anger comes from you and it is your own creation.

> A Zen student came to Bankei, a Japanese Rinzai Zen master, and complained: 'Master, I have an ungovernable temper. How can I cure it?'
>
> 'You have something very strange,' replied Bankei. 'Let me see what you have.'
>
> 'Just now I cannot show it to you,' replied the student.
>
> 'When can you show it to me?' asked Bankei.
>
> 'It arises unexpectedly,' replied the student.

> 'Then,' concluded Bankei, 'it must not be your own true nature. If it were, you could show it to me at any time. When you were born you did not have it, and your parents did not give it to you. Think that over.'

Let us understand anger and master it. By knowing the nature of anger, we can avoid its creation itself, which would make our lives peaceful and happy. Even if sometimes anger is created within, we can find a safe passage to release it and avoid the harmful consequences of an angry mind without losing our happiness.

18

Acquire True Knowledge

To know that we know what we know, and to know that we do not know what we do not know, that is true knowledge.

—Nicolaus Copernicus

This world works according to certain laws that have been laid down by nature and by the government. Some rules are well-known like the law of gravity that provides us the exact amount of force exerted on any object by Earth and accurately predicts the exact speed at which you will land on the ground if you decide to jump from a tenth-floor apartment. Nature makes no distinction here whether a saint has jumped or a sinner, as everyone would fall on the earth with the same speed. In the same way, laws of the nations also provide definite punishment for certain crimes.

Every seed buried under the soil grows and bears fruits according to the law of nature. It is not possible for a tennis ball to move upward if you drop it from your hand nor is it possible for the seed to bear fruit the next day of its getting planted. Everything moves in this world according to some rules and ignorance of these rules is the cause of our failures and misery.

A person who takes responsibility of his life believes in the immutability of laws that govern this world. When we fail to achieve our desired fruit, it is because we failed to sow the right seed in the right soil at the right time. If you throw the best of the seed on a rock, nothing would come out of it. In the same way, if you wish to eat mango in your own orchard today, you must have sown its seeds a few years ago.

Hence, if you are not happy today, it is because you have not performed the right actions at the right time in the past. If you wish to have any fruit, you must have the ability to identify the right seed, right soil and the rules of nature that are responsible for the growth of the seed. We need true knowledge to predict and create our future. True knowledge has the followings elements.

Knowing the Self

You are reaping today what you have sown in the past and what you sow today would be ripe in the future. You are the seed of tomorrow. It is important to know yourself. You must know the minutest details about yourself.

- You must know what you like, what you dislike and 'why'?

- You must know whom you like and whom you dislike and 'why'.

'Why' is extremely important because while the people and things you like or dislike may be different, the 'why' is common. You may like people for some reason and the knowledge of that reason is the true knowledge of your self. For example, you may like people because they are beautiful, honest, hard-working, rich, successful, selfless or due to some other reason. In the same way, you like writing, reading, playing, talking or travelling for some reason or the other.

What you like and dislike tells you what you are.

Knowing the self is the greatest wisdom, because when you discover yourself, you also discover your source of happiness within.

Knowing the People

'Don't go around saying the world owes you a living,' said Mark Twain. 'The world owes you nothing. It was here first.' The world is what it is. Just like you can't wish gravity away, you can't wish people away if you don't like them. The evils and goods of this world are interconnected and often complementary.

- There are rich people, because there are poor people.
- There are sinners, because there are saints.

Remove all the laws of the world and lo! There is no crime and no criminal in the world. Everyone becomes a good citizen just like there is no crime in a jungle, since there is no one to judge or brand an act as a crime in a forest.

The world is not going to change according to our worldview. You have the option of wasting your life by cursing the world, or enjoying it by understanding and accepting it as it is.

When you accept the world as it is, you also accept yourself as you are. One who wants a perfect world has to start with accepting himself as a perfect self. It is not easy. Even making yourself perfect is great torture. Changing the world, of course, is an impossible task. Even Gods, Prophets and Avatars could not change the world.

However, it is possible to change yourself and change 'your' world. Your world consists of a small number of people like your family, friends, relatives and colleagues. By living peacefully with them, you can surely make your world better. If you are still left with more energy and life, then you can try and change the rest of the world.

Knowing the world means having first-hand knowledge about it, which in turn means understanding 'why the world is what it is' and 'why people are what they are'?

You know the world by knowing the people in it. Knowing the people does not mean giving an adjective to everyone such as good, bad, selfish, selfless, honest or liar because every person is a combination of the opposite qualities in different proportions. You will never find anyone a complete angel or a devil, as angels and demons, both together, make up a person's personality.

When you know a person thoroughly, you know the cause of his behaviour and by influencing the cause you can change the behaviour of the person.

Knowing the Rules

When you try to understand the world from your experiences, you start discovering hidden rules that govern the world. You start noticing a pattern in the behaviour of men. The world gives back what you give to it, but not in the same proportion and not immediately. Every action of yours follows a trajectory and you land up exactly in a place where you should arrive according to the rules of the world. Your ignorance of the rules will not change your destiny.

In order to understand the rules of the world, you must learn to connect the effects with the causes. If your result is not as expected, it is not due to some divine forces or the destiny written in your palms, but because you don't know the rules of the game. You must have the courage to accept your ignorance or the error of your judgment to discover the right rules. Once you know the right rules, you can take the correct decisions and perform the appropriate actions to achieve the desired goal.

You can learn these rules from books, from the learned people and also from your life experiences. Once you develop awareness of the world and develop the habit of learning from your own successes and failures, each experience of yours will automatically teach you the rules of the game called life.

Trusting Yourself

The famous management guru Peter Drucker has said, 'The best way to predict your future is to create it.' You create your future by possessing the right knowledge and taking the right action at the right time. You need patience, knowledge and faith to create your future. You become smarter with every action you take today and move a few inches closer to your desired goal. When you are able to predict and create your future, you develop trust in yourself, in other people and in the rules of life.

When you trust a person, you believe in his words and actions. A trustworthy person will not promise what he can't deliver. However, you can't deliver what you promise, unless you know yourself, know others, know the rules of the world and take the right action at the right time. Stephen Covey rightly said, 'Trust is the glue of life. It's the most essential ingredient in effective communication. It's the foundational principle that holds all relationships.'

Happiness is the result of a positive experience of our inner world with the outer world, which in turn creates trust between us and the world. True knowledge is original and objective. It is in harmony with the fundamental principles of the world. These principles can't be written or spoken but can only be known through experience and practice. You can use such knowledge to solve all types of real-life problems. When you repeatedly deliver what you promise, people trust you and you become trustworthy. You develop the ability not only to predict your future but also to create it due to your deep understanding of the world. You also learn to identify who is trustworthy and who is not. You don't get disappointed with people who can't be trusted and who don't keep their promises, as you never expected them to fulfil their promises in the first place.

True knowledge is thus the key to happiness. However, you can't have such knowledge merely from books or by listening to scholars. True knowledge comes only by experiencing life and connecting the dots. When you are aware and your mind is disciplined, true knowledge flows from all directions into your being.

19

Balance the Opposites

Without contraries is no progression. Attraction and repulsion, reason and energy, love and hate, are necessary to human existence.

—William Blake, English poet and painter

'I maintain that Truth is a pathless land, and you cannot approach it by any path whatsoever, by any religion, by any sect,' said Jiddu Krishnamurti, one of the greatest philosophers of India. He added further, 'The moment you follow someone, you cease to follow Truth.'

Happiness, like Truth, is a pathless land and there are no prescribed methods to achieve it. However, many experts have tried to provide people with ready-made formulae for happiness. They claim they can show you the way to happiness as if it is a destination that can be reached by following a prescribed path. However, in most cases, when you follow that path, you hardly arrive at the promised land of happiness. Your life may become even more miserable now because your path to happiness might have taken you to a land even farther away from it. George F Will, an American newspaper columnist, journalist and a Pulitzer Prize winner has said, 'To visit a bookstore is to feel misgiving about universal literacy, which has produced mass market for hundreds of profoundly sad handbooks on achieving happiness.'

There can't be any formula for happiness because happiness is an effect and not a cause. The same activity, which at one time gave you happiness, may now become a source of suffering. Or often a great suffering ends up becoming a source of joy.

Nature creates everything with a purpose and nothing is redundant in this world, even though it may not be desirable to you. Good and evil are not really opposite to each other, but complementary to each other like man and woman. Both the genders exist in the world in almost the same numbers. In the same way, when society tries to create 'goodness' of any form, an opposite of good, that is, 'evil' is also created in the world to balance the goodness. Imagine a society, where everyone desires only a male-child and prays to God only for male children, and God really starts listening to all their prayers and the society bears only male children. There is no price for guessing that such a society would collapse soon.

We, however, can't stop dividing the world into two—one desirable and the other undesirable. For example, good is desirable while evil is not; love is desirable but hatred is not; selflessness is desirable but selfishness is not; non-violence is desirable while violence is not; life is desirable but death is not.

In our minds, we have done such a clear division of the world that half of the world is holy, good and desirable, while the remaining half is profane, unholy and undesirable. We have not even spared animals. Hindus consider cows to be so holy that it is compared to a mother but the value attached to the lives of other animals is not the same. Killing a cow is the greatest sin that a Hindu can commit but the people of other religions can kill the same cow, without calling sin upon themselves and enjoy beef, as a regular food item. In the same way, a pig is considered to be so unholy for Muslims that some of them do not even utter the word pig. Yet there are millions in this world who relish pork.

When you avoid half of the reality of this world, you lose all balance of life and also your happiness. Imagine standing on one foot all the time! There is no single thing in the world that contains everything we would need. Even with food, we need to eat a variety to get different nutrients for good health. Hence, we have to assimilate different things to get a balanced diet for happy living.

Balancing the Opposites

It is important to understand that everything in this world is relative and everything exists with respect to each other. A man is considered short because others are taller and a man is considered tall when others are shorter than him. Short and tall are relative to each other and have no significance in absolute sense. This Supreme Truth is revealed in *Tao Te Ching*, a Chinese classic text:

When the world knows beauty as beauty, ugliness arises
When it knows good as good, evil arises
Thus being and non-being produce each other
Difficult and easy bring about each other
Long and short reveal each other
High and low support each other
Music and voice harmonise each other
Front and back follow each other

Your happiness depends on your ability to balance the opposites rather than sticking to only one of the truths while ignoring all others. When you avoid something for long, over a period of time, it creates a craving in you that can disturb the peace of your mind and make you suffer immensely. For example, if you skip a meal, your mind will be thinking of food. In the same way, sex too is a basic need of human beings. If you ignore sex, soon your mind gets filled with the thoughts of lust and you lose all happiness.

A happy person does not discard anything and takes a balanced approach to life by accepting the opposites. He never allows even his body to be deprived of anything. Let us examine some of the opposites whose balancing is extremely important for happiness.

Cooperation and Competition

Most people consider competition bad because it causes conflict. Cooperation is considered to be good as everyone gets benefited when people cooperate with each other. Bruce Lipton, an American developmental biologist, who is best known for promoting the idea that genes and DNA can be manipulated by a person's beliefs, once said, 'Nature is based on harmony. So it says if we want to survive and become more like nature, then we actually have to understand that it's cooperation versus competition.'

The world, however, can't survive exclusively either by cooperation or by competition. If there is no growth without competition, there is no love and peace without cooperation either. Extremes of both are unhealthy. A happy man is one who learns to balance these two extremes. He competes with his rivals and yet does not lose compassion for them.

Selfishness vs Selflessness

You are considered to be wrong if you are selfish and right if you are selfless. In reality, there is no person who can be absolutely selfish or selfless. You can't be selfless without being selfish. You can't give anything to another person, unless you first earn it yourself. Hence, the act of giving is intimately connected with the act of earning. The more you take from the world, the more you can give. Bill Gates is the most charitable person in the world today because he has also taken the most from the world.

Self-interest is important for self-negation. You can achieve success only when you appeal to the self-interest of people. Napoleon Hill, an American speaker and motivational writer, has said, 'If your imagination leads you to understand how quickly people grant your requests when those requests appeal to their self-interest, you can have practically anything you go after.'

It is not bad to be selfish as your first responsibility is to take care of yourself. Only when you are satisfied and happy, you can make others happy and become selfless.

Attachment and Detachment

We find two opposing philosophies about happiness. When we love someone, we are extremely happy but we also get attached to our beloved. This attachment is considered to be the root cause of all our miseries. Bhagavad Gita says, 'While contemplating the objects of the senses, a person develops attachment for them, and from such attachment lust develops, and from lust anger arises. From anger, complete delusion arises, and from delusion bewilderment of memory. When memory is bewildered, intelligence is lost, and when intelligence is lost, one falls down again into the material pool.'(*Gita 2:62-63.*)

Buddha also considered attachment to be the root of all sufferings. A true Buddhist is a monk, detached from all worldly things and pleasures. Yet, it is difficult to live in this world without love and attachment. Max Muller aptly said, 'A flower cannot blossom without sunshine, and man cannot live without love.'

While love is a great source of happiness, it can also become a great source of suffering if not balanced properly. You have to give space to your beloved to have a loving relationship with her. Extreme love suffocates. A man who loves everyone suffers immensely as he develops attachment towards everyone and hence his pains are also multiplied. A happy man is one who balances attachment and detachment well so that his happiness is maximised.

Duality in Harmony

The key to happy life is to develop the ability to balance the dualities that exist in the world. When you understand that there is nothing really good or bad in this world in the absolute sense, you focus your attention on balancing everything in the appropriate manner rather than craving for something and discarding the rest. A happy person, like a healthy person, takes a balanced diet of everything that nature presents to him.

In the harmonious synthesis of the opposite ends of the river, flows the stream of happiness.

20

Deposit in Your Happiness Account

The greatest degree of inner tranquility comes from the development of love and compassion. The more we care for the happiness of others, the greater is our own sense of well-being.

—Tenzin Gyatso, the fourteenth Dalai Lama

Imagine that someone pickpocketed you on your way to home and you lost hundred thousand rupees that happened to be the total saving of your life. You would be extremely upset. You may shout at the government for not maintaining law and order, curse the pickpocket or cry at your misfortune. You may even go into depression.

Now imagine that you have two hundred thousand rupees more in your bank account. You will surely feel the pain of losing hundred thousand rupees but still the pain would be bearable. Now imagine that you have ten million rupees in your bank account. The lost amount is just 1 per cent of your accumulated wealth and may not be even equal to one month's interest income that you earn on your savings. Now the loss of hundred thousand rupees would pinch you even lesser. Even if you are disturbed due to the loss of your money, you would still be fine within a few hours. You will perhaps learn from this experience and take precautions to ensure that such mishaps do not occur in future.

The Happiness Account

We all face problems in life that disturb our peace and make us unhappy. While some people crack up under unwanted and unexpected situations, others are able to overcome their suffering much more easily. This is possible for those who have developed the ability to withstand adversity due to positive balance in their happiness accounts. We must have the ability to withstand the bad times to be able to enjoy the good times. If you can't survive your sufferings, you can't enjoy your blessings.

We come across all types of people in our life—some are happy, some are unhappy; some are optimistic and some are pessimistic; some are honest and some are crooked. It is not possible for you to avoid all negative people and negative situations. Also, there is no way you can avoid some people, who may give you pain and sorrow intentionally or unintentionally. We sometimes suffer not due to our fault but due to the faults of others.

Every bad experience is a source of unhappiness. Yet the intensity of suffering can be controlled. Just like a person who has a million-dollar bank balance is likely to get less disturbed due to loss of a few dollars, you too can easily overcome some bad incidents in your life, without losing much joy, provided you already have a great amount of happiness in your life.

Imagine a bank where you can make deposits of your happiness. Let us call this bank Happiness Bank. If you make regular deposits in your happiness bank account, your balance will increase. Now, when you face some unexpected situation or a painful experience that makes you lose some happiness, you withdraw from your account but remain calm and cool because there is still sufficient balance in your happiness account.

Exchange Surplus in Your Happiness Account

We know how to do transaction of material things. We buy products from the market and each product has a price. So we pay money equivalent to the price of the goods or services and acquire them. Similarly, we can sell some goods and get money in return. Or we provide services to an individual or an organisation and get a value of our service in cash or kind. Now imagine two situations:

- What happens when we take something from the world and refuse to pay for it?
- What happens when we give something to the world but don't take anything in return?

When we take something and don't pay the price for it, we are punished by the world for fraud, crime or corruption. Such punishment gives us pain in proportion to what we have taken illegitimately from the world.

However, when we voluntarily refuse to take anything from the world while sharing what we have with it, we get praise and honour in return, and that gives us joy.

This is the simplest way of creating happiness in this world. All such selfless actions add to your happiness and increase the balance in your happiness account.

Happiness is a result of the exchange surplus you create with the world. The more you give to the world and the less you take from it, the more surplus you create and that adds to your happiness balance. There are several ways to increase your happiness balance.

Material Exchange

Money is highly valued in the material world because you can buy all material things from it. People try to earn more money so that they can make their lives comfortable and secure their basic needs like food, water and shelter. Each one of us, even the richest, spends our wealth carefully trying to get maximum goods and services in exchange of the money we have. We bargain hard to get the best deal for our money. However, when you spend money on someone without expecting anything in return, you get spiritual equivalent of your wealth in the form of happiness. Charity and the act of giving are enshrined in every religion as a great spiritual act to please God. The Bible says:

> Then the King (Lord) will say to those on his right, 'Come, you who are blessed by my Father; take your inheritance, the kingdom prepared for you since the creation of the world. For I was hungry and you gave me something to eat, I was thirsty and you gave me something to drink, I was a stranger and you invited me in, I needed clothes and you clothed me, I was sick and you looked after me, I was in prison and you came to visit me.'
>
> Then the righteous will answer him, 'Lord, when did we see you hungry and feed you, or thirsty and gave you something to drink? When did we see you a stranger and invite you in or needing clothes and clothed you? When did we see you sick or in prison and went to visit you?'
>
> The King will reply, 'Truly I tell you, whatever you did for one of the least of these brothers and sisters of mine, you did for me.' (*Matthew 25:34-40*)

Giving wealth, however, does not automatically bring happiness, unless it is given to the right person willingly and without any expectations. Bhagavad Gita explains the three types of charities:

- **Sattvik (Nature of Truth)**: Charity given as a matter of duty, without expectation of any result, at the right place and time and to the right person. (*Gita 17:20*)
- **Rajsik (Nature of Passion)**: Charity given either in the hope of receiving in return, or with a view to winning merit, or grudgingly. (*Gita 17:21*)
- **Tamsik (Nature of Darkness)**: Charity given at the wrong place and time and to the undeserving

recipient disrespectfully and with contempt.
(*Gita 17:22*)

The purpose of charity is to help a person lead a better life. When you give charity to a wrong person, you don't help him but rather spoil him as he misuses the money that causes him more harm than good.

In the same way, when you earn wealth by doing things that are not conducive to the society, you pay from your happiness account. People, who are doing illegal or immoral things in their professions, are constantly depleting their happiness account. Thieves, dacoits, fraudsters and corrupt people can make huge amounts of illegal money through elicit activities. However, they have to pay spiritually by losing their happiness and suffering from inner guilt throughout their lives.

Karmic Exchange

While it is difficult to choose the right person at the right time for charity, helping someone directly without expecting anything in return can hardly go wrong. Mother Teresa's selfless service to thousands of people had given her so much happiness that she devoted her entire life in helping others. We too can gain happiness from our small acts of kindness.

Your random acts of kindness like helping a blind man cross the street, giving free tuition to poor children or cleaning your surroundings, never go waste as they get deposited in your happiness account. If you refuse to accept any remuneration for your good work, you enrich yourself spiritually by getting more joy in your life.

Emotional Exchange

We are creatures of emotions. We love some people and dislike others. Most people exchange love just as they exchange goods and services, on quid pro quo basis. We love those who love us and hate those who hate us. Jesus Christ asked people to love even their enemies:

> You have heard that it was said, 'Love your neighbour and hate your enemy.' But I tell you, love your enemies and pray for those who persecute you, that you may be children of your Father in heaven. He causes his sun to rise on the evil and the good, and sends rain on the righteous and the unrighteous. If you love those who love you, what reward will you get? Are not even the tax collectors doing that? And, if you greet only your own people, what are you doing more than others? Do not even pagans do that? Be perfect, therefore, as your heavenly Father is perfect. (*Matthew 5:43-48*)

A wise person hates none and loves everyone. When you give love to someone without any expectations, your happiness account is credited. Each time you hate those who love you, or cheat your friends or become unfaithful to your beloved, a certain amount of happiness gets debited from your account.

If you are filled with hatred, you can hardly enjoy genuine happiness. Hatred makes your personality extremely fragile and you lose your temper on the slightest pretext, which further creates enmity. That is why Gandhiji said, 'An eye for an eye only ends up making the whole world blind.' One, who is burning in the fire of revenge, can hardly be a happy person.

Deposit Regularly in Your Happiness Account

One of the best ways to achieve a happy life is to make regular deposits in our happiness account and withdraw as less as possible. This will be the best investment of your life. If you have sufficient balance in your happiness account, it can take care of the unexpected losses. The richer your happiness account is, the more you are insured against unhappiness from other sources.

Ronald Reagan once said, 'Peace is not absence of conflict; it is the ability to handle conflict by peaceful means.' A man with ample happiness balance is peaceful even in difficult situations as he can always withdraw happiness from his happiness account. He is peaceful in the same world where most people are miserable because they have not accumulated enough in their happiness account.

21

Invest in Suffering

Character cannot be developed in ease and quiet. Only through experience of trial and suffering can the soul be strengthened, ambition inspired and success achieved.

—Helen Keller

We often consider suffering to be the opposite of happiness. We all wish to avoid suffering and do what gives us pleasure. However, it is almost impossible to avoid suffering all the time since it is so widely spread in our world.

Once we understand that suffering is unavoidable in human life, we can find ways to reduce and minimise our sufferings rather than try to run away from them.

Suffering is relative just like heat is relative. If you put your hand in a glass of water at normal temperature after putting it first in hot water, it feels colder. The same water would feel hotter, if you have put your hand first in cold water. We enjoy ordinary food when we are hungry, but the same food becomes tasteless, when our stomach is full.

Nature ensures joy and pain to everyone. When you are only expecting joy in your life, you can't handle pain and any painful episode will seem to be even more painful to you. However, when you are mentally prepared for pain, it can't make you suffer easily. If most people suffer, it is because they are always expecting pleasure and happiness in their life. Hence, when suffering knocks at their door, they are unprepared for it and suffer immense pain.

In one study, a few volunteers received a series of twenty electric shocks and were warned three seconds before the onset of each one. Some volunteers (the high-shock group) received twenty high-intensity shocks. Other volunteers (the low-shock group) received three high-intensity shocks in between seventeen low-intensity shocks. Although the low-shock group received shocks of fewer volts than the high-shock group, their heartbeat was faster, they sweated more profusely and they rated themselves as more afraid. Why? Because volunteers in the low-shock group received shocks of different intensities at different times, which made it impossible for them to anticipate their future. Apparently, three big jolts that one cannot foresee are more painful than twenty big jolts that one can.

This study establishes that when we are mentally prepared to receive pain, the impact is much lesser as compared to when we are unaware of the impending pain.

Accepting Pain

Once we accept that suffering is a part of life, we not only reduce its impact but may also transform it to joy. When suffering is unwanted, it is a source of pain. When suffering is voluntary for a desirable purpose or associated with a sacred act, it ceases to be a source of pain and becomes a joy. Most people find morning walks extremely boring and unpleasant, though everyone knows the benefit of walking. However, if you develop the habit of walking every morning, it may become such a pleasant activity that you would not like to miss it. Some people get so used to morning walks that they walk even when it is raining, albeit with an umbrella. Walking can become such an integral part of your life that you may get addicted to it. You would start missing it just like an alcoholic misses his drinks. Yet it is a good addiction because it provides you with many health benefits.

Reading also seems to be a painful activity in the beginning to some people. It is often forced upon you by your parents. However, when you start to read and enjoy books, it becomes one of the most pleasant activities of your life.

It is painful when someone insults you in public. However, you can develop immunity even from insults by thinking rationally. A wise man is not affected by insults hurled at him by others. The Roman stoic philosopher Seneca said it aptly, 'Wise man...says to himself, "Do these things befall me deservedly or undeservedly? If deservedly, it is not an insult, but a judicial sentence; if undeservedly, then he who does injustice ought to blush, not I".'

The joys that come from transformation of the self are much more durable than the joys derived from sensual gratifications like eating, drinking or indulging in sexual activities.

You are transformed and purified through the sufferings, chosen voluntarily, for achieving a greater purpose in life. Kahlil Gibran rightly said, 'Out of suffering have emerged the strongest souls; the most massive characters are seared with scars.'

How Does Suffering Transform People?

Sufferings are painful when we don't want them. Once we decide to welcome sufferings as a means to achieve higher goals of life, they become a source of joy. We as human beings can enjoy helping others, fighting for our country, fulfilling our responsibilities as parents, praying to God, visiting pilgrimages and even waking at night for the sake of our children.

We have to cultivate these sources of joy with great effort over a period of time. A student can study twelve hours a day or a scientist can work eighteen hours a day if he enjoys what he is doing.

Our animal instincts can be compared with weeds that grow naturally but often harm the useful crops.

Our human qualities are like the beautiful lawn or the fields of paddy. They don't grow naturally but need human effort for growth. They bring pleasure to the world.

When we suffer for a greater cause, we are transformed into a superior human being. When you practise weight-lifting in a gymnasium, your body gains strength, your heart becomes stronger and your mind becomes more disciplined.

If you are forced to go to the gym for a workout against your wish, you are unlikely to enjoy it even if you are building muscles. Similarly, a student who is forced to study twelve hours a day by his parents does not become knowledgeable even after spending all his waking time with books. However, when we want to read books voluntarily and force ourselves to study; our mind and soul start undergoing slow transformation. Our actions gradually transform our thoughts.

When you develop a regular habit of going to a temple, library or a gymnasium, you start liking these activities as your thoughts are transformed. You would also undergo similar changes, if you start visiting brothels regularly.

Once your mind and soul are transformed, even the most difficult actions start flowing naturally from the simplest of human beings. Lord Krishna says in Bhagavad Gita: 'All actions are entirely done by the qualities born of the nature of the soul. However, man deluded by his ego thinks, "I am the doer".'(*Gita 3:27*).

By doing the things that are noble, we become noble and by doing the things that are evil, we become evil. James Allen, a British philosophical writer, has said: 'A noble and God-like character is not a thing of favour or chance, but is the natural result of continued effort in right thinking, the effect of long-cherished association with God-like thoughts. An ignoble and bestial character, by the same process, is the result of the continued harbouring of grovelling thoughts.'

Transform Sufferings to Joy

When we suffer for good, we become good from inside and then our sufferings come to an end because we start deriving pleasure in suffering for a good cause. Such transformation brings permanent joy in our life because we not only enjoy the pleasures, which are available to all human beings due to our basic instincts, but we can also enjoy the pain that is detested by people.

Abraham Lincoln once said, 'Do I not destroy my enemies when I make them my friends?'

When you develop friendship with suffering, it becomes your source of joy.

Is it not the best way to eliminate suffering from your life?

22

Tune in with the Rhythm of Life

Happiness is not a matter of intensity but of balance, order, rhythm and harmony.

—Thomas Merton, American theologist and mystic

There are many views on happiness and many experts talking on it. The methodologies suggested by some of the experts may even work some time for some people. However, as you continue to follow these methods, you soon start to realise their futility. Often these methods become a source of pain rather than provide you any real happiness.

There is no formula for happiness. Yet none of the formulae of happiness are wrong.

In order to understand happiness, let us draw an analogy between the mystery of happiness and the mystery of songs.

A song consists of poetry and rhythm. While poetry consists of words in a structured manner, rhythms are indefinable and unique. When you listen to a song, the words are captured by your mind, while the rhythm is experienced by your heart. There is no reason why you like a particular song, yet you find some songs magical and memorable while others don't leave any imprint on you.

The rhythm of music is made by seven notes and five sub-notes that are arranged in a unique sequence. Rhythms are harmonised with the lyrics of the song to create the magic. In a good song, it becomes extremely difficult to decide if the music was created for the words or the words were written for the music as they perfectly blend together.

Now imagine that instead of using all seven notes, you use only one note.

Can you create any music by pressing just one key of the piano?

We know it is impossible.

To create a beautiful piece of music, you have to use many notes in a unique and rhythmic manner. If you randomly mix the notes, you can't create a melodious song.

In the same way, a beautiful and joyful life can't be created by following any principle or dogma or by following all the principles in a random manner. You have to learn the art of harmonising all the principles of happiness in a way that matches the rhythm of your life and creates happiness for you.

The Rhythm of Time

Many gurus and experts advise us to learn to live in the present in order to enjoy happiness. However, it is not possible to be always in the present, as our mind is constantly thinking about the past and the future.

In order to bring lasting joy to our lives, we must harmonise the past, the present and the future. We must think about the past, be in the present but also visualise our future in a harmonious rhythm. When all three time dimensions are present in our life, we enjoy peace and happiness.

There can be no formula about how much time we must spend in the three dimensions of time. Sometimes we have to be in the past for a long time to learn the lessons the past has to offer. Sometimes we have to devote a substantial amount of time to the future and plan ahead, while sometimes we need to just stay in the present to execute those plans. It is only by practice that you know how much time you must devote to the past, present and future in order to catch the rhythm of time.

The Rhythm of Feelings

We are told that love is good and hate is evil. We are also told that love comes from God while hatred comes from Satan. Hence, we are advised to love everyone, including our enemies. It is, however, impossible to love everyone.

- How can you love a person who has raped and killed an innocent girl?

- How can you love a person who has brutally murdered an innocent citizen because he belonged to a different religion or caste?

The fact is that all emotions have a purpose in life and nothing should be considered better or inferior than the other in all situations. There are numerous emotions such as love, hatred, fear, anxiety, guilt, grief, anger, surprise, happiness, boredom, lust, compassion and each has an important role to play in our lives. We need to feel and go through all the emotions in our lives. While we may not desire some of them as they can cause pain, their absence can't complete our lives either. Why should you not feel guilty if you have done something wrong? Guilt too has a purpose as it prevents you from committing the same or similar inappropriate, immoral or illegal acts again in your life. Guilt purifies and transforms us. There are several criminals who changed for the better once they were purified by their guilt.

We need to feel all the emotions as they appear without preferring one over the other. When we give preference to one and block out the way for the rest, we create imbalances in our emotions which eventually destroy our joy. When you forcefully stop yourself from hating, hate mounts with time and one day, when it bursts, it takes you by surprise and you end up committing great crimes.

The Rhythm of Action

Many people are always busy in their lives doing something either to earn more money or to acquire power.

They work long hours in office, keep themselves busy on their mobile phones or laptops. Even when they go on vacations, they take their phones and laptops along. People have a tendency to keep themselves busy in doing so-called useful things in life. For them, enjoyment means parties, where they dance, drink and network with others.

Inaction is an anathema for many people because they believe that time is money and wasting time is wasting money. According to them, why should you sit idle or waste your time talking to your friends, watching movies, or listening to your favourite songs, or simply sleep long hours, when you can use the same time for doing something productive?

Wise men, however, know that action and inaction are not different. In Gita, Lord Krishna says, 'One who sees inaction in action, and action in inaction, is intelligent among men, and he is in the transcendental state, although engaged in all sorts of activities.'

There are three types of activities.

1. Actions to make a living
2. Actions to enjoy life
3. Inaction to relax and sleep

Let us divide the twenty-four hours of the day in three equal parts consisting of eight hours each. We should broadly spend eight hours working at our jobs to make a living, eight hours in doing what we enjoy and the remaining eight hours in relaxing and sleeping. The division is not mechanical and hard-coded. For example, we often work for five days and get two days off and then we have more time to relax and enjoy. We sometimes, take leave from work and go on vacation, where we get more time to relax and enjoy life.

The need for weekends and vacations arises because we don't adequately relax and enjoy our life on most days of the week. What we need is to try and harmonise all three types of activities. You must work-enjoy-relax in a rhythmic manner. For example, you may focus on your work for some time and then relax a little, and then continue your work again. Or mix pleasure with job by cracking some jokes, talking to a friend or sharing the personal problems of your team members. There are no fixed rules for deciding the rhythm of life but you would know instinctively when you are on the right track. If you experiment, you would understand the rhythm of your life and start enjoying your work, leisure and entertainment.

When you are overworked, you crave for enjoyment and leisure. You are gripped with the TGIF (Thank God It's Friday) phenomenon. When you fail to relax during the week and end up using all your weekend leisure time to catch up on your sleep instead, you get MMB (Monday Morning Blues). A harmonised life is one, where everything is so balanced that there is no craving for anything. You can love work, entertainment and leisure by harmonising them with each other.

The Rhythm of Gratification

We feel happy when we satisfy our cravings, but these cravings change from time to time. For example, you crave for sleep after a hard day's work, and after you have slept peacefully at night, you want action. When you are hungry, you crave for food. But once the hunger is satisfied, you want to work.

We often think that only money, power and comfort give us gratification. But this is partial truth. We also feel happy when we play, work out, solve a complex problem or make a child smile by our love and affection. We enjoy success and hate failure, but there is hardly any success that is not preceded by failure. It is our failures that make our successes sweeter.

Our gratifications are physical, mental, emotional and spiritual in nature. Even within each category, there are several types of gratifications. For example, physical gratification is not only sex or good food, but also working-out, walking, playing or swimming. If you have sensual pleasures for a long time, you lose the ability to enjoy pleasure. But when pleasure follows pain, it seems much more pleasant. An air-conditioned room feels more satisfying after a walk in sultry weather.

In the same way, if you are only reading what suits your taste, you would soon get bored. You must also read books that are not as per your taste, even if it means putting in great effort in the beginning to read such books. It is only when you force your mind to exercise itself by reading difficult thoughts that it grows, similar to the situation where the muscle mass in our body increases when we lift weights. When you broaden your mind, your ability to enjoy reading increases.

Let us try and understand the rhythm of gratification through our cycle of eating food. We usually take three meals: breakfast, lunch and dinner at approximately 9 am, 2 pm and 9 pm. So the time difference between the meals is around 5 hours, 7 hours and 12 hours approximately. This time gap is determined by the quantity of food taken at the previous meal time and the work we perform following that meal. Since we sleep at night, the gap is more while the gap is less when we are active during the day. Now if you increase the food intake without changing your schedule, you are likely to feel bloated. If you reduce the food intake, but continue with the same routine, you are bound to feel hungry. The right combination of food is one which leaves you neither hungry nor feeling overstuffed till your next meal. This harmony should come naturally. For example, if you had a heavy dinner, you must take light breakfast, or if you have taken a heavy breakfast you must go in for lighter lunch. If you have been physically active during the day, you may need more calories to replenish your energy.

If your rhythm of eating is in tune with your activities, you will enjoy good health and feel good all day. However, if you don't care for the signals coming from your body and eat according to a fixed schedule in fixed quantities, you may feel uncomfortable and even spoil your health.

Catching the Rhythm of Life

I was interested in learning how to play guitar during my college days. Initially I was asked by my teacher to practise a few standard notes so that my fingers get attuned to the instrument. Once I became comfortable playing the standard notes in a fixed sequence, I learnt a few simple songs. After I played a couple of songs on the guitar, I gradually started developing a sense of music. And one day, I played a new song all by myself. With more practice, I was able to play more complex songs without referring to any notes. My fingers would automatically find the right notes and the song would be played out as naturally as I could sing a song.

The same holds good for understanding any form of rhythm. It is only by practice that you can understand the events of life and find the right rhythm. Once you get into the rhythm of life, you can flow with life and enjoy happiness effortlessly.

23

Forgive and Forget

The weak can never forgive. Forgiveness is the attribute of the strong.

—Mahatma Gandhi

What happens when someone attacks you physically or through hurtful words? You get wounded. The physical wounds give you physical pain and the verbal wounds give you emotional pain. Physical pain can get healed in some time with proper medical treatment, but emotional wounds rarely get healed. Most people want to pay back the offender in the same coin. Our desire for retaliation is best stated in the Bible (Old Testament): 'If there is serious injury, you are to take life for life, eye for eye, tooth for tooth, hand for hand, foot for foot, burn for burn, wound for wound, bruise for bruise.'

When we have succeeded in wounding the offender

in the same manner as he had done, we feel relieved. However, if the offender is far more powerful than us, or is a family member, elder or our loved one, we can't retaliate and the wound remains inside our heart.

As we grow in our life, our heart becomes a reservoir of wounds that were given to us by different people during the course of our lives. Even when we have wounded others, we create a wound within ourselves due to our feeling of guilt. If you had injured a person by running him down with your car a few years ago but managed to flee from the spot incognito, the wound stays in your heart in the form of guilt created by imagining how much pain the injured person would have suffered and his curse on you. Suppose, you have shouted at your child or at your mother at some point in the past, you know that your actions have caused deep hurt to them. You will always feel guilty whenever you think about the incident. Even though years may pass, you fail to forget the incident because the wound given by you is still living in your heart and mind.

Sometimes the person who hurts you continues working with you and you have to deal with him everyday. The moment you see the person, the wound is scratched again and you suffer the pain yet again. When a wound is scratched repeatedly, it becomes even more painful and requires more attention to get healed.

You can't have happiness if your body and mind are wounded. You have to find a method to stop creating new wounds and heal the existing ones.

Forgiving Yourself

Everyone in this world is connected in a spiritual space. We can't hurt others without hurting ourselves. The more you hurt others, the more wounds are created in you because the whole world is like one organism of which you too are an integral part. You often don't realise or acknowledge it, because acknowledging that you have hurt others is enough to create pain in you. However, when you are silent and alone, you can't help but feel this pain for which you know you are responsible.

We hurt other people sometimes deliberately and sometimes unintentionally. For example, when you are travelling on the road, you may be killing several ants and insects that are moving on the road and you may not even be aware of it. On the other side, you may kill millions of insects purposely with an insecticide spray. We often hurt the feelings of our subordinates in our desire to get work done efficiently and achieve our targets. Sometimes, we deliberately pressurise, ridicule and criticise our subordinates because we feel that they would not perform otherwise.

We lose our temper when our subordinates don't perform their work according to our expectations. We lose our temper easily when we know that the other person can't hit us back. We rarely lose our temper before our bosses, valuable clients, or powerful people in spite of great provocation. Our temper immediately gets annulled when we are pitted against a person more powerful than us.

One day a man who was drunk, and at a football game, was making such a nuisance that people around him threatened to call the police if he didn't sit down and shut up.

At that he shouted—'Show me a policeman, and I will show you an idiot.'

No sooner the words were spoken than a big six-foot policeman arrived on the scene and said, 'I am a policeman. Now show me the idiot.'

'Great!' said the trembling man, 'I am the idiot!'

Once my boss lost his temper in an important meeting where several senior officials from other departments were also present. He had always been nice to me and had never lost his temper before. I was extremely hurt and felt deeply humiliated. However, in the evening he came to my room, where I was preparing a presentation for a seminar to be held the following week. He sat with me for more than two hours, helping me prepare the presentation. Even though he did not formally apologise, I knew that he was feeling sorry for his behaviour. I forgave him. Soon my anger was gone and so was my hurt.

I then realised that there are several ways of saying sorry and you must choose a way which suits you the most. When we are angry, we don't realise how our actions are hurting others. Hence, allow the temper to cool down and your rational mind to be back in control again. Only when you are peaceful, you can analyse your actions and know its impact on others. Once you have realised your mistake, take steps to remove the hurt in whichever way possible.

If you have humiliated someone, you can heal the hurt by praising him. For example, if you have reprimanded your child for something, it would be advisable to sincerely praise him at the next best opportunity. Your praise should not be perfunctory or superficial. You must make a genuine effort and spot the good things about your child that can be praised whenever the right opportunity arises.

There may be some people you may have hurt who are either no more alive or you don't know where they are anymore. For example, if you have said something hurtful to your grandfather or grandmother and they have passed away, how will you heal the wound now? In such situations, it is advisable to admit your fault to God and before people whom you love and trust. The *Bible* says, 'Confess your sins to one another and pray for one another, so that you will be healed. The prayer of a good person has a powerful effect.' *(James 5:16)*

If the people you hurt are still around, you can seek their forgiveness by admitting your mistakes. You can also ensure that you talk to them regularly, praise them in private and in public so as to ameliorate the effect of the bruise on your heart. Slowly you will find that the wound within you is healing and you are free from the pain.

When others have caused hurt to you, you can also heal yourself by forgiving them. Jesus Christ has said, 'If you forgive others for the wrongs they have done to you, your Father in heaven will also forgive you. But if you do not forgive others, then your Father will not forgive the wrongs you have done.' (*Matthew 6:14-15*)

Forgiving Others

We are often more aware of the wounds received by us than the ones we have given to others. When we see a person who has hurt us, our wound gets refreshed and our pain resurfaces. Whenever that person is discussed, our hurt resurfaces. When that person is praised by others, our wound becomes even graver. Many people carry so many wounds in their heart, from so many people, that they can't sleep peacefully at night.

The wounds need not be from the people whom we know personally. Sometimes we are greatly hurt by a leader whom we trusted and voted to power; sometimes by the salesman who sold us a defective piece of equipment. We are hurt by our loved ones, by our enemies and also by strangers. Our nature is such that we can forget a thousand blessings but remember every hurt.

A minor pain in one part of body is enough to destroy the joy derived from wellness of the rest of the body. When you give a talk, you may get appreciation from hundreds of participants. However, if one participant criticises your lecture, you remember that criticism more than all the appreciation.

Pain is always more powerful than pleasure, especially when it pertains to us. However, when it comes to others, we reverse the rules.

- We don't remember the numerous wounds we have given others, but remember every act of charity and goodness we did for them.
- We take for granted the good deeds done to us by others but we remember every act that hurts us.

It is not easy to forgive and forget others unless we develop proper understanding of the self and the world. If you wish to heal yourself, you must understand other people's perspective. Try and focus on the good things a person did for you before reminding yourself of his hurtful deeds. When you balance the good and the bad, it is much easier to forgive.

However, there may be situations when there are hardly any good deeds done by a person who has hurt us. In such situations, try to understand the person as he is. If he is someone who rarely does good to others, you must develop sympathy for him because he is like an unwell person who has numerous wounds in his own heart. A happy person can share happiness and an unhappy person can only share his miseries.

You share what you have and not what you lack. When someone is infected with a virus, he infects everyone who comes close to him. When the same person becomes healthy again, he stops spreading the virus. You don't blame a sick person for spreading virus as you understand that he himself is in terrible pain because of the illness caused by the virus. Doctors don't kill the patient for being sick, but cure him so that he becomes healthy again.

You must treat an evil-doer in the same spirit as a doctor treats a patient and develop sympathy for him. It is better to maintain distance from unhealthy people and protect yourself rather than become intimate with them and later curse them for infecting you with their viruses.

However, when you are hurt by a person who is usually good to others, you must introspect. If you have been hurt by a majority of people around you, they all can't be wrong. There is a good possibility that you yourself are at fault.

> A woman went to a doctor and complained of pain in all parts of her body.
>
> She touched her forehead and screamed with pain. She touched her stomach and again cried with pain. Whenever she touched any part of the body, she cried with pain.
>
> The doctor after carefully examining her found the source of pain.
>
> She had a wound in her finger.

The healing of wounds is a slow process and needs continuous efforts and practice. However, once you develop the right habits, which do not create new wounds either in you or in others, your old wounds start healing and you become healthy and happy once again. There is a lot of wisdom in the words of Maya Angelou, American poet, singer and civil rights activist: 'It's one of the greatest gifts you can give yourself, to forgive. Forgive everybody.'

Forgive and Let Go

When you forgive someone completely, you must also get rid of all the bad memories. Unless you forget such incidents, the wound in your heart is not healed and it becomes sore if scratched by you or by anyone else. The real benefit of forgiving comes when you completely forget the wound.

Forgiving is mutual. When you forgive others, you are also forgiven by them. Phillips Brooks, American clergyman and author, has said: 'Forgive, forget. Bear with the faults of others as you would have them bear with yours.'

Once you develop the habit of forgiving, you would soon find that you do not feel hurt anymore because the same understanding which helps you forgive, helps you in not getting hurt in the first place. You can easily avoid such situations in your life that cause you or others hurt and pain. Just like a healthy body is not easily infected by external bacteria and viruses, a healthy mind too is not easily infected by external insults and undesirable events. Lewis B Smedes, author and theologian, said wisely, 'To forgive is to set a prisoner free and discover that the prisoner was you.'

Learn to forgive and forget to free yourself from all the pain and miseries of the past.

24

Develop the Habit of Giving

Happiness...consists in giving, and in serving others.

—Henry Drummond, Scottish Evangelist

It is impossible to be happy alone in this world even if you are the mightiest and the richest person in the world. You need other people to share your love, joy and success. There is a constant flow of thoughts and energies between our inside world and the outside world, and the experience of this exchange is the source of our pleasure or pain.

We know that our body temperature generally remains around 37 degrees Celsius. If the atmosphere is very cool, we lose some heat from our body and we feel chilly. A chill can be a source of pain, if it is excessive but can be a source of joy at a more pleasant temperature, which is estimated to be around 22-25 degree centigrade. This is what an air conditioner does—it maintains a constant temperature in the room, irrespective of the outside temperature.

Just like the body needs to give a part of its energy to the world to get comfort, we need to give a part of our material and emotional energies to the world to experience joy. H Jackson Brown, Jr rightly said, 'Remember that the happiest people are not those getting more, but those giving more.' The joy of giving is at its best when the material gifts are given with love. However, some people find it impossible to give anything to others.

> A very rich lawyer is approached by a famous charity organisation. The man from the organisation is concerned that the lawyer made over ten million dollars last year but didn't donate even a cent to the charity.
>
> 'First of all,' says the lawyer, 'my mother is sick and dying in the hospital and it's not covered by healthcare. Second, I have six kids through three divorced marriages. Third, my sister's husband suddenly died and she has no one to support her four children...'
>
> 'I'm terribly sorry,' says the man from the charity organisation, 'I feel bad asking for money.'
>
> The lawyer responds, 'Yeah, well if I'm not giving them any money, why should I give you any?'

There is no price for guessing that a man with such a mindset would be terribly unhappy even if he were the richest person of the world.

All relationships are based on giving. We can't create everything by ourselves to fulfil our requirements. The national and international trade of goods and services ensures that people give what they have, in exchange for something they lack.

The practice of exchange has given rise to a variety of relationships between human beings. You also exchange happiness, feelings and love in exchange for something else. When you stop giving, you cut yourself off from the world and all relationships gradually come to an end. Even Gautam Buddha, who discarded his kingdom and his family to become the Enlightened One, shared his wisdom through his sermons.

A man may produce just one thing or give just one service, but may get other things he needs from the world, by sharing his own product or service. We too can get everything that we need to make us happy by giving what we have in abundance. When we give something the world needs, it also gives us back what we need. This exchange creates a virtuous cycle that enhances our joy manifold.

There are many things that we can give to others:

Wealth

A famous proverb says, 'When wealth is lost, nothing is lost; when health is lost, something is lost; when character is lost, everything is lost.' It may be true because wealth can always be regained even after a loss. However, when you lose health, it is difficult to regain it. Character is something, which once lost, can never be redeemed.

Yet many of us value wealth more than anything else. People work long hours, take lots of tension and suffer much humiliation only to make more money. Wealth is important in life just as food is important for sustenance of the body. Yet excessive accumulation of wealth, like excessive consumption of food, only leads to misery. It is wealth that creates enemies and often is the most important reason for crimes like abduction or murder.

The uneven distribution of wealth is one of the main causes behind crimes in the world. There are people who are billionaires while there are billions who are unable to earn even one dollar a day. There are millions of people today who are going to bed hungry every night, have no medical facilities and no home to live in, due to their poverty. When we give part of our wealth to them, it makes them happy without diminishing our own happiness.

The incremental value of wealth declines as we become richer. Yet people keep on accumulating it. They think that more is better. Hence, when they fail to get happiness even after becoming wealthy, instead of looking for the appropriate reason for their unhappiness, they blame lack of greater wealth for the lack of happiness and work even harder to make more money with the hope of buying happiness with money.

Giving can give you joy only if it is given with love and without any expectations. Bernard C Meltzer, American radio talk show host, said, 'We may give without loving, but we cannot love without giving.' When you love others giving becomes so natural that you can't withhold it.

Time

Time is wealth, which is fairly distributed to all creatures. All of us have exactly twenty-four hours every day. If one gives his time to someone, he loses that much of time permanently from his life. So the gift of time is equal to the gift of life.

You have to spend time to enjoy any form of happiness. You need time to visit the most beautiful places of the world. You have to have time to enjoy a movie, a cricket match or play golf. How you distribute your time determines how you shape your life.

When you give your time to someone, you enhance their happiness. Even the most secure relationships don't survive if the couples don't give enough time to each other. Giving time to your friend, children, family and colleagues can greatly enhance your happiness. However, care must also be taken to spend time with yourself so that you understand and know yourself and become a happy and loving person. Swami Vivekananda had said, 'Talk to yourself once a day…otherwise you may miss meeting an excellent person in this world.'

Appreciation

Most people are good at criticising others. They can run down anyone if given an opportunity. However, there are only a few who can look at the positive side of others and appreciate their good qualities. Ralph Marston, a writer and publisher of *The Daily Motivator* had once remarked, 'Make it a habit to tell people "thank you" to express your appreciation, sincerely and without the expectation of anything in return. Truly appreciate those around you, and you'll soon find many others around you. Truly appreciate life, and you'll find that you have more of it.'

We are liberal in criticising but miserly in praising others. We spend our appreciation even more miserly than we spend our wealth. The result is that we also don't get any appreciation from others.

- When we don't appreciate others, we gradually fail to see the positive side of other people.
- When others don't appreciate us, we fail to see the positive side of our own selves.

When we learn to see goodness in people, we appreciate them naturally. People who appreciate little also see little goodness in others. We can train ourselves to see the positive side of every person. When we develop the habit of appreciating others, they too appreciate us. This creates a virtuous cycle of appreciation in which there is mutual respect and admiration. We all feel very happy when our work is recognised and we are appreciated by others. Dale Carnegie said, 'Be hearty in your approbation and lavish in your praise, and people will cherish your words.'

The Joy of Giving

You must plan your life in such a way that at the time of your death, you own nothing, and have given everything. You can't carry anything with you to the other world and everything shall be left here in this world after you are gone. All that will remain of you will be your good work.

Once a rich man approached a famous saint and requested him to ensure his place in heaven. He wanted to pay any amount of money for this work.

The saint smiled and gave him a small needle and asked him to give that needle to him in heaven.

The rich man said, 'How can I carry a needle to heaven?'

Then the saint smiled and said, 'If you can't carry a small needle to heaven, what is the value of all your wealth in heaven?'

We have come in this world empty-handed and will go from this world empty-handed. Hence, it would be better if we give the world everything we have earned from it. This is only a fair and just proposition. The greatest advantage of giving back to the world is that you get happiness and love from the world in return even without asking for it.

25

Count Your Blessings

I just find myself happy with the simple things. Appreciating the blessings God gave me.

—DMX, American rapper and record producer

We are so accustomed to comparing ourselves with a better person that we often don't realise how much goodness we possess ourselves. We don't pay attention to what we have but focus on what others have. Often, our mind is engaged in thinking about what we failed to achieve in life and what we still don't have. The result is unhappiness and frustration.

A man was extremely poor. He decided to end his miserable life. He climbed the highest cliff and was about to jump when a saint stopped him at the last moment.

'What are you doing?' asked the saint.

The man started crying and said that he is very poor and he owns nothing.

The saint told him, 'But you are already a millionaire.'

The poor man thought that the saint was making fun of his poverty and hence said, 'Why are you ridiculing my poverty?'

The saint said, 'OK! I can prove that you are a millionaire.' The man readily agreed.

The saint said, 'There is a rich man who needs a kidney. If you give one to him, he can give you Rs 5,00,000. You anyway have two.'

The man thought for some time and then refused to part with his kidney. The saint then asked him to give one eye for one million rupees. The man refused him again. Thus, the saint asked him to give other parts of his body by telling him the market price of the limbs but the poor man refused every offer one by one.

Then the saint counted the value of all the body parts and proved that the poor man was indeed a millionaire. The poor man realised his mistake and then started working with all his vigour and soon became a rich man.

We are all like this poor man and fail to recognise our own worth.

- If you have full hair on your head, you take it for granted. There are thousands of bald people, who would be willing to pay any amount of money to get hair restored on their heads.
- If you are healthy and you can eat anything, it is of no importance to you. However, one who is suffering from diabetes and is prohibited from

eating many food items, would be willing to pay anything to eat the food of his choice.

There are so many things which we have but have not paid any attention to them. If only we can learn to appreciate our blessings, we can enjoy great happiness.

Count Your Wealth

If you have not already done so, please count all the wealth that you have earned in your life. Also aggregate your investments. Now calculate the minimum expenditure that is required for you to manage a decent standard of living. For most of us, the expenditure on food is hardly a fraction of our earning. If you decide to cook your meals at home, you can afford to eat nutritious food at a very affordable price. Think of your requirement for a house. We all live only in one bedroom, however big the house may be. The size of the bedroom is also not very significant. As long as a bed can fit in it, it is sufficient. If you can't afford a house in a posh locality, you will still have enough to afford it in a suburban area.

Consider how wealthy you are as compared to billions of people in the world, who earn less than a dollar a day and are not even sure where their next meal will come from. If you have a sound mind and healthy body, you can surely earn enough to live a decent life and also save something for the future. If you learn to lead a simple life, you can live within your means, happily. Mahatma Gandhi described in his autobiography *My Experiments with Truth* how he changed his habits to simplify his life:

> I had started on a life of ease and comfort, but the experiment was short-lived. Although I had furnished the house with care, yet it failed to have any hold on me. So no sooner had I launched forth on that life, I began to cut down expenses. The washerman's bill was heavy, and as he was, besides, by no means noted for his punctuality, even two to three dozen shirts and collars proved insufficient for me…so I equipped myself with a washing outfit to save it. I bought a book on washing, studied the art, and taught it also to my wife. This no doubt added to my work, but its novelty made it a pleasure.
>
> In the same way, as I freed myself from slavery to the washerman, I threw off dependence on the barber. All people who go to England learn there at least the art of shaving, but none, to my knowledge, learns to cut their own hair. I had to learn that too…
>
> The extreme forms in which my passion for self-help and simplicity ultimately expressed itself will be described in their proper place. The seed had been long sown. It only needed watering to take root, to flower, and to fructify, and the watering came in due course.

When you reduce your needs, your income and wealth multiply by default. What looked small earlier seems big now and you become a rich man in your own eyes even though your wealth remains exactly the same in numerical terms.

Count Your Health

One of my uncles told me an interesting incident. He was attending a marriage party of an influential person in a famous five star hotel. The owner of the hotel was also present in the party. When everyone started choosing the most exotic and mouth-watering food from the numerous cuisines laid out, the owner simply took soups and salads on his plate. When my uncle asked him to take more and try other cuisines, he said that the doctors have severely restricted his diet due to his many ailments. My uncle told me that the first thought that came to his mind was how unfortunate the owner of the hotel was. He was feeding thousands of people everyday but he himself could not enjoy any of those foods. How is he any better than a person who does not have money to pay for the food?

Most of us, however, don't consider being healthy as a blessing. We don't appreciate that we can enjoy eating everything. It is only when we lose our health and become sick that we understand the joy of health. If you are healthy, you can enjoy good food, enjoy your work and have a nice sleep at night. Don't spoil your health by excessive use of your body, overeating, intoxicants or drug abuse. Love your body and love your life and thank God for giving you a healthy body.

Count Your Love

We are all blessed with love right from the day we were born. Everyone loves a child even though a child can't give anything back to them except his smile. However, his smile is worth more than a fortune for his loving parents.

Love is most essential for growth of a human being. A child needs not only food but also love for growth.

However, most people fail to appreciate love as they grow up. We take love for granted and think that it is the responsibility of our parents, siblings, spouse and children to love us for what we are. If you are a person who is still loved by your loved ones, you are indeed a blessed person because there are millions of people in the world, who have lost their love in accidents, negligence or carelessness.

Love and faith are interconnected. If there is no faith, there can't be any love. Even the most intimate love can't withstand the onslaught of adultery, lying and cheating. Once you lose your love, it can never be brought back. If your beloved loses faith in you, it can never be restored.

Learn to value your love before you lose it.

Count Your Work

Most people are dissatisfied with their jobs and wish they didn't have to go through the drudgery. Many people find other people's jobs more interesting. They wait for weekends, holidays and even retirement to enjoy their lives.

Remember the joy you felt when you got the appointment letter of your first job? How excited you were to get the job and become financially independent? Even now, there are millions of people who may be trying to get a job like yours. However, you stopped appreciating the value of your present job as you have taken it for granted.

Imagine that you get fired from your job because of some reason. How difficult it would be to get a new job? You can't even be sure if the new job would be more or as interesting as the present one. You may also have to relocate. You may not even get a job. How are you going to sustain yourself and your family?

> One day Mullah Nasruddin saw a man sitting in a pall of gloom. When asked the reason for his sorrow, the man replied that his life had become so miserable that he had collected all his money in a small bag and was wandering around seeking happiness.
>
> All of a sudden, Nasruddin picked up the man's bag and dodging him disappeared from his sight. The man was running all around to catch Mullah and get the bag back, which was his only possession. After some time Nasruddin placed the bag at a place, where the frantic man could see it and then hid himself behind a tree. When the man found his bag, he forgot his grief and began dancing with joy.
>
> Mullah murmured, 'This is one way to bring happiness to a sad man!'

If you imagine the worst case scenario, you will easily be able to appreciate your own blessings of what you have. A job is not merely a means to earn livelihood but it also gives you a position in the society. You also participate in the betterment of the world by making meaningful contribution through your profession. Whether you are collecting taxes, policing the city, selling soaps or coding a programme, you are doing something for the society and you are also supporting your family with the income. If you focus on the larger role you play, while doing your job, your suffering would be greatly reduced and you will feel proud of your job and yourself.

Count Your Blessings

If you start to count your blessings, you will start to notice what you have more than what you don't. While it is good to be ambitious and strive to be more prosperous in your life, it is also important to be grateful for what you have. If you can't enjoy what you have earned, you can never be happy. When you are focused on what you have, you have no time to bother about what others have.

Count your blessings and be happy with what you have.

26

Restrict Your Options

I may be running out of options, but running out isn't an option.
—Mark Lawrence, British-American author

One of the better things about the modern world is the availability of numerous options in almost every field. If you are visiting a restaurant, you can get dozens of varieties of food and drinks. A good ice-cream parlour will overwhelm you with the numerous options of ice-cream flavours it stocks. You have the option to change your religion and even change your citizenship. You have thousands of options of dresses in a supermarket. You can find millions of books listed on online portals such as Amazon, Flipkart, etc. and you can choose anything you wish to read.

The advent of internet has multiplied our options to learn, interact and socialise. While in the earlier days, you could make friends only with people living in your neighbourhood, today you can make friends in any part of the world. There was a time, only a few decades ago, when the governments of different countries restricted harmful materials like pornography and provocative literature from being sold in the country, but today everything is available online without any geographical restrictions.

In earlier times, people used to feel settled when they got a job or married their beloved. However, today you have the option to change your mate and change your job anytime, if you are not happy with them.

Ideally speaking, availability of options should make the life of modern generation much more enjoyable as compared to their ancestors, who had little or no options. However, in reality, people are more miserable today than ever.

When you have multiple options and you can choose only one, you often feel unhappy about discarding the rest of the options, when your chosen option does not provide you happiness and satisfaction. Also, when you have multiple options, you never feel settled since you are always moving from one option to another, one person to another and one job to another which ends up making your life more miserable than enjoyable.

Loss Aversion

In order to understand why our life becomes more miserable when we have more options, we must understand the concept of *loss aversion*. This concept was first identified by economists Amos Tversky and Daniel Kahneman.

Daniel Kahneman was awarded the 2002 Nobel Memorial Prize in Economic Sciences for his discovery.

His studies have suggested that losses are twice as powerful psychologically, as gains. It means that one who loses Rs 10,000 will lose double the amount of satisfaction in comparison to the satisfaction a person gains by getting Rs 10,000. For example, if you make two investments, in one investment you made a profit while in the other you made a loss of the same amount, the pain due to loss of investment is much more than the gain made by the other investment, though the net loss or gain is still nil to you. Hence, if we choose among two equally good options, the pain of losing one is more than the joy of gaining the other. Our loss is more than our gain unless what we have chosen is twice as good as the option that is lost, which is rarely the case.

In the real world there are many competing options which differ from each other only fractionally, so people suffer more by remembering their losses than by relishing their gains.

Restricting Your Options

In the ancient times, people followed religion when taking many decisions in their life. Religion usually doesn't give you many options.

- You follow only one Supreme God.
- You follow only one religion.

When you have no options, your attitude towards life changes. For example, if you believe that you have only one soulmate in the world and you can fall in love only once, you don't think about loving another person in your life, fearing that it would amount to betrayal of your soulmate.

Similarly, if you get married and you have no option of a divorce, you would try to resolve all the disputes by finding a solution of the problem rather than trying to find fault in each other or blame each other for sabotaging the relationship.

It is for this reason that in religions like Hinduism, which does not sanction divorce, there are far less instances of divorce, even though the law now permits it. It is due to this belief—that you get married only once—the rate of divorce in India is less than 1 per cent while it is almost 50 per cent in the Western world where the option of divorce is exercised freely.

Synthetic Happiness

It is common for people to associate happiness with success. When we get what we want, we feel happy. When we don't, we have reasons to feel unhappy. Most people are unhappy since they fail to get what they want in life. However, even when they actually get what they want, their happiness is short-lived because very soon they raise the bar to a higher level and again start struggling to achieve the next level. Their happiness level thus comes back to the original level as before.

We can, however, create happiness synthetically by redefining happiness itself.

In a Ted Talk on Synthetic Happiness, Dan Gilbert,

American businessman, mentions how we can create our own happiness and how it's like a 'mental immune system'. In one experiment, when students were given the choice to choose one of the two best pictures:

- They liked the picture they retained/chose more if the choice was irreversible
- They liked the picture less when they had the option to re-decide their choice after four days

Hence, when we close our options at some point of time, we learn to be happy with what we have. However, when we keep our options open, we are rarely happy with what we have as we find the grass greener on the other side of the fence.

You don't have to get your object of desire to be happy. You can be just as happy even if you don't get what you want. You can manufacture your own happiness by accepting what you have and believing that what you have is the best. Such manufactured happiness is called 'synthetic happiness'.

The freedom to choose is the friend of natural happiness but enemy of synthetic happiness. The best way to create synthetic happiness is, therefore, to restrict your options to as few as you can. Synthetic happiness acts like our psychological immune system and helps us be happy even in adverse situations. We change our views of the world, so we can feel better about the world we find ourselves in. It works best when we're totally stuck, when we are trapped.

Increasing Your Happiness

One of the best ways to achieve happiness in life is to restrict your options. The more options you have, the more pain you may suffer.

You can reduce your options by developing faith and genuine love. You consider options only for the material things and not when you are emotionally attached to someone. No person would like to exchange his children even with the most beautiful and intelligent children of the world because love makes everything invaluable and irreplaceable.

In the same way, religion makes even an ordinary activity sacred and immutable. When you consider marriage as a sacred act, you don't think of breaking it up for any reason. Once you have made up your mind to stay with your partner, whatever it takes, you shall find a way to resolve all disputes that crop up between you two.

When you start viewing the world with love and compassion and find the same soul inhabiting in every person, you can lose the materialistic vision of people and things. Your options are naturally reduced to minimum, which helps you multiply your happiness.

27

Maintain the Right Stress Levels in Your Life

It's not stress that kills us, it is our reaction to it.

—Hans Selye, Hungarian-Canadian endocrinologist

Most people dream of a life that is free of problems and challenges. This happens because we assume that problems and challenges are unwarranted and cause us pain. Hence, most people prefer comfort and peace in life. Millions of people wait for retirement when they would be free from all the stresses of their job. Ernie J Zelinski, the international bestselling author and speaker, found this desire prevalent in a large part of the population, 'Retirement is supposed to be the great escape from the stresses inherent in most jobs, a time to experience a fulfilling life derived from many enjoyable and rewarding activities.'

However, most people hardly enjoy their life once they retire. They often get bored when they don't have much to do. Their passion for doing thousands of things post-retirement soon peters out and the comfortable and workless life starts to appear monotonous.

You enjoy comfort more when you are tired. If you are always living in comfort, it loses its value in your life and often becomes a source of pain.

Only those retired people manage to live happy lives who don't shun work even after retirement. The famous author Wallace R Curiel has written, 'There is not a single healthy retired person I know who does not still work to one extent or another—even if he or she does not need the money, including me! Why? Because even if you don't need the money, you still need the work!'

Work is important in life because without work, we are useless on this planet. Our actions connect us with the world and give a purpose to our lives. We feel valued when we do something for the society. Benjamin Disraeli, the former prime minister of UK said it aptly, 'Action may not always bring happiness; but there is no happiness without action.'

And when there is action, there is stress.

Importance of the Right Stress

When we play a musical instrument like guitar or violin, we often adjust the stress or tensions in the strings by tuning the instrument. If the tension in a string is too high, the music created by the instrument is shrill and becomes out of tune. If the tension is increased even more, the string may break and no music will be created from such instrument. If the tension in the string is too less, the instrument is again out of tune and it won't be able to create pleasant music.

In order to enjoy music from any instrument, you require to manage the right amount of tension in its strings and tune it properly.

In the same way, in order to enjoy happiness in our lives, we have to create right amount of stress in our lives. Such stress is useful for building strength and leads to better performance. This stress is often called eustress or good stress. The eustress is required at physical, mental and emotional levels.

Physical Stress

Your body seeks comfort. It wants to relax more and work less. Most people find it quite difficult to get up early morning. However, they are forced to get up because they have to go to office or catch up on the morning chores. Often parents have to persuade and nag their children constantly to leave the bed. Most people work because they have to work to earn money and live a decent life. Although, they hate doing what they have to do. When you start your day with resentment, you are unhappy almost the whole day.

Instead of seeking comfort for the body, you should seek discomfort for it. This can be done by getting up early and going for a walk or to the gym or doing some workout or yoga at home. There is bound to be some resistance from your body since it does not want to work hard. However, once you force your body to do what is good for it, it becomes stronger and soon it develops more muscle and stamina.

When you are accustomed to working hard, your body soon gets so used to it that it starts feeling uncomfortable if it is not pushed to work. People who are used to early morning walks, often feel disheartened if it rains heavily in the morning and they can't go for their walk. People who are used to working out in a gym can't miss their exercise even for a day.

When you develop the habit of voluntarily putting yourself under stress, it becomes a source of joy and even comfort. You feel happy, satisfied and relaxed after the workout. The best thing is that you lose fear of physical stress because you have started enjoying it.

Mental Stress

Just like our body wants comfort, our mind too wants relaxation. It wants entertainment and stimulation rather than learning and thinking. Your mind has the solution to all your life's problems provided it thinks hard. Voltaire, a French enlightenment writer, said wisely, 'No problem can withstand the assault of sustained thinking.'

When the mind gets lazy, it does not wish to think. It does not wish to exert itself to find solutions to life's problems. When you want your mind to work, it finds excuses not to work and often asks you to consult some expert for the solution rather than striving on its own.

Be a master of your mind and force it to work even if it does not wish to. Soon you will find that your mind is much better than what you had expected it to be, as it can provide many solutions to the problems of life. Robin Sharma, Canadian writer and motivational speaker, explained this nicely when he said, 'The mind is a wonderful servant, but a terrible master.'

When you force your mind to solve difficult problems of life, it soon starts feeling good due to its ability to solve them. It develops deeper thoughts and its intelligence gets sharpened. It is so energised that it wants to take even more problems and solve them, even if they pertains to others.

Once your mind is thoughtful and confident, you stop bothering about the problems of your life as you know that you will be able to solve any problem that confronts you. Buddha has said in his discourses, 'We are shaped by our thoughts; we become what we think. When the mind is pure, joy follows like a shadow that never leaves.'

Emotional Stress

We are connected with the world through our feelings and emotions. Emotions are the cause of love and hatred. They make our world heaven or hell. However, most people find it difficult to handle emotions as they have no control over them. Sometimes, we love a person and that person does not reciprocate our love and affection. We feel pain and unhappiness in such a one-sided love. We feel small and humiliated when we are rejected by others.

When we are in a relationship, we have to fulfil

its obligations. These obligations sometimes tire us and we feel stressed labouring constantly under their burden. Relationships also make us weak as our happiness depends on the people whom we love, like or admire. Hence some people avoid relationships to avoid the emotional stress associated with them. Oscar Wilde, playwright and author, has written in one of his texts, 'I don't want to be at the mercy of my emotions.'

People often avoid having a conversation with strangers or trusting other people. They don't want to take any chance in the matter of relationships. They want to be left alone and avoid all emotional stress.

It is important to build a little stress in your life by trusting new people, making new friends and nurturing new relationships. It is possible that some of them would turn sour over a period of time and some of the people whom you trusted would betray your trust. However, many relationships would turn out to be much better than expected and they are enough to compensate for the loss of the ones that did not work out.

You also develop the ability to suffer break-ups and betrayal, when you are engaged in relationships. Once you get the ability to overcome such emotional stress, your heart becomes stronger and you can develop better ties with others.

Come Out of the Comfort Zone

It is good to enjoy a comfortable life for a while. However, the enjoyment derived from comforts magnifies when it follows stress. When you are tired with the hard work of the day, you get better sleep at night. When you voluntarily create stress in your life, it becomes a source of joy for you rather than becoming a source of pain. Stress becomes a problem, only when it crosses a limit and becomes unbearable.

It is wisely said, 'A comfort zone is a beautiful place, but nothing ever grows there.'

It is only when we come out of our comfort zones and build the right amount of stress in our lives, can we enjoy happiness by tuning our life with the rhythm of the world.

28

Nurture Your Potentialities

A man of vision cannot question his potentials. He does not doubt his capabilities. He keeps going because he had seen himself gone already in his visions.

—Israelmore Ayivor,
Inspirational author and blogger

Imagine that you go to a ready-made garments shop. This shop has clothes of one size, one colour and one design only. When you ask the shopkeeper to give you a shirt of your size and shape, he refuses saying that their only product has been designed according to the size of the best man/woman of the world. He then tells you that you should change yourself to fit into the shirt-size than expect the shirts to be altered to fit you. He tells you that you are underweight or overweight, tall or short and the problem is with you and not with the shirt. If you ask for a shirt of any other design or colour, he again asks you to change your views and preferences because he has kept only the best colour and best design in his store.

We know that such absurd one-size-fit-all formula does not work in the real world. In the same way, it is not possible to have a one-size-fit-all formula for happiness. What works for one person may not work for another. Everyone has to choose his own methods to achieve happiness.

Power of Potential

We all enjoy different things in life. People find success and joy in different activities such as reading, writing, speaking, playing, serving, singing and other things, because each has a different potential. Mother Teresa enjoyed serving people while Adolph Hitler was the complete opposite. What we like defines us. Let us explore why we like what we like.

Alexis Carrel, a French surgeon and biologist, who was awarded the Nobel Prize in Physiology or Medicine, explained the concept of potentialities in men in his book *Man the Unknown* as following:

> Every human being is born with different intellectual capacities. But, great or small, these potentialities require, in order to be actualised, constant exercise and certain ill-defined environmental conditions. Intellectual power is augmented by the habit of precise reasoning, the study of logic, the use of mathematical language, mental discipline, and complete and deep observation of things. On the contrary, incomplete and superficial observations, a rapid succession of impressions, multiplicity of images, and lack of intellectual discipline hinder the development of mind.

When we work upon our potentialities in the right way, they grow and become a source of joy and success. However, most of us are not even aware of our potentialities because we never test them. If you have a great potential to become a writer, but you have never practised writing as a craft, your potential remains hidden and you can't enjoy writing as a joyful activity.

We develop different types of potential based on our environment and profession. Sometimes, these traits come to the forefront in an adverse situation. For example, Mahatma Gandhi could realise his potential of becoming a great leader when he was thrown out of the first-class railway compartment in South Africa due to racial discrimination. When he was humiliated, instead of taking things lying down, he decided to fight back the racial discrimination using non-violent methods and gradually became one of the greatest leaders of the twentieth century.

During the Nazi occupation of the Netherlands, Anne Frank received a blank diary as a present on her thirteenth birthday. She began writing two days later. Her family had to go in hiding within a couple of days. They remained hidden for two years but they were discovered and deported to a Nazi concentration camp, where they died. Anne Frank, however, wrote her experiences in her diary, which was later published as a book: *The Diary of a Young Girl*. This book is so beautifully written that it has inspired many plays, and has been adapted as a movie and included in several top-books lists of the twentieth century.

She too discovered her potential as a writer in extremely adverse situation.

Discovering Your Potential

Your potential is a hidden treasure. You may not be even aware of it till you discover it. However, it is not easy to find your potential when you are following others or trying to achieve success in an area which is the most sought after. Most people in the modern world are part of the rat race and they are trying to win the race just like others. They have no time to discover who they are and what they love to do.

Albert Einstein once said, 'Everybody is a genius. But if you judge a fish by its ability to climb a tree, it will live its whole life believing that it is stupid.' Most people lead miserable lives because in their attempt to win the rat race, they try to excel in the area for which they don't have the potential. Hence, they fail not only in achieving success, but end up making their lives miserable as well.

It is therefore not surprising that most people discover their potential accidently under adverse situations. However, you can't plan accidents and hence you can't rely on them to know who you are and what your true potential is.

The right way to discover your potential is to experiment in life as much as possible. When you experiment, you will either succeed or fail. Either way you learn something about yourself and the world and become wiser. Every experiment proves something. If it does not prove what you intended originally, it proves something else.

Mahatma Gandhi has admitted it, 'I have nothing new to teach the world. Truth and non-violence are as old as the hills. All I have done is to try experiments in both on as vast a scale as I could.' It is only through experiments that Gandhi improvised thousands of years old principles of non-violence of Jesus Christ and Buddha to create the movement that finally led to the independence of India from the British rule.

Realising Your Potential

It is not enough to only discover your potential. Your potential, at best, is like a rock from which the statue is yet to be carved. A rock of raw diamond can't be used to make rings and the dust of gold is useless for all practical purposes. Only by honing your skill through hard work, you can develop your potential and achieve happiness and success in your life.

Malcolm Gladwell, an English journalist, author and speaker, in his book *Outliers: The Story of Success* examines factors that lead to high levels of success. He examines the life of great men such as Bill Gates and gives the '10,000-Hour Rule'. He claims that the key to achieving world-class expertise in any skill, is, to a large extent, a matter of practising the correct way, for a total of around 10,000 hours. Even though there is no scientific study to prove the efficacy of this theory, it can't be disputed that you need enough time to develop a skill that can put you above others.

Most people don't have the patience to work for so long and they want success soon. This does not happen because even if you are doing an act that is truly world-class, people will not recognise your work till you constantly do the thing with excellence for such a long time that you acquire world-class reputation. A brilliant piece of writing by an unknown author is not even noticed, while the ordinary work of a well-known author becomes a bestseller. It is worth remembering that even this well-known author had to struggle, like an ordinary author, at the start of his career when he was not that popular.

Cristiano Ronaldo, the best soccer player of the year, decided to test if people can recognise his skill without recognising him. He dressed up as a homeless man—including fake hair, beard and clothes, before taking to the streets with a dog and football. In the busy Plaza de Callao in downtown Madrid, he started doing kick ups. No one gave him a second glance. To everyone else in the Plaza, he just looked like a homeless guy trying to earn a few euros from the locals. Occasionally, passers-by would stop to watch the homeless man's impressive football skills, especially when he replicated Ronaldo's trademark step overs, but that was that. Several hours passed before a kid decided to play with him and the two took part in a bit of one-on-one before Ronaldo gave him a hug (still dressed as a tramp), picked up the ball and signed it. The young boy looked perplexed, wondering why this man had signed the football and that was when Ronaldo began to peel off the disguise, leaving his new best friend open-mouthed and on the verge of tears. Needless to say, everyone in the

Plaza, who had previously ignored what they considered to be a tramp, suddenly flocked to the scene, mobile phones in hand.

Nurture Your Potentials

Our lasting happiness comes by doing what we are best at. You can know what you are brilliant at only when you discover your potential. If most people remain unhappy throughout their lives, it is because they fail to know their real potential and nurture it to make it a source of joy for themselves. They keep searching for the source of happiness in the outside world, while the real source of happiness is hidden within them.

> Once a man found Mullah Nasruddin searching for something on the ground outside his house. On being asked, Nasruddin replied that he was looking for his keys. The man also joined in the search and in due course asked Mullah, 'Where exactly did you drop them?'
>
> Mullah answered, 'In my house.'
>
> 'Then why are you looking here?' the man asked.
>
> 'There is more light here than in my house,' replied Mullah.

You have to discover the key of your happiness inside you and not outside as your potential to achieve success and joy lies within.

29

Develop Intimate Relationships

I believe that two people are connected at the heart, and it doesn't matter what you do, or who you are or where you live; there are no boundaries or barriers if two people are destined to be together.

—Julia Roberts, Hollywood actor

In the civilised world, there are severe restrictions on speaking your mind. Every law passed by the Legislature restricts our freedom in some way or the other. It is getting more and more difficult in the modern world to express your feelings and emotions freely. You can't shout, you can't get angry even at your children whom you love deeply. You could be jailed for calling a thief a thief, a corrupt a corrupt or even a murderer a murderer if you don't have evidence to prove the same before the courts.

We need people with whom we can share our intimate

feelings and thoughts. If you have no one to share your thoughts and emotions with, your mind gets burdened with them. The need for sharing your heart and soul leads to relationships that connect you with the world.

In order to understand the need of a relationship, let us try to understand the need for clothing. Every person is nude beneath the clothes. However, it is impossible to imagine a civilised man without them. Mark Twain has said, 'Clothes make the man. Naked people have little or no influence on society.'

Yet we don't wear the same clothes on all occasions.

In schools, children are required to wear uniforms. The purpose behind the requirement is that schools don't wish to discriminate children based on their attire and hence ask all of them to wear the same uniform.

The uniform is usually discarded when you go to college. You are now free to choose your dress and wear it as far as it is socially acceptable. Colleges promote the ideology of freedom and creativity and a uniform is not going to be consistent with that thinking.

You go to your office dressed in formals. Formals can be interpreted in different ways in different organisations but still what is 'formal' is broadly defined. For example, many offices won't allow you to wear T-shirts or shorts or slippers.

Your dressing at home usually doesn't change much. At home, you wear clothes that are comfortable rather than those that are fancy or expensive. Clothes for home may include shorts, slippers, pyjamas or sleeping suits. We have different dresses when we visit the market, go to a five-star hotel for dining, go to the gym or go for a party. How strange will you look if you wear pants, shirts and tie at home or wear shorts or pyjamas to office?

Even though we remain the same person, we have different types of relationships with our parents, children, spouse, relatives, friends, teachers, students, colleagues and neighbours. Each type of relationship fulfils a need which other relationships can't fulfil.

A happy person is one who maintains all types of relationships in life.

The Spectrum of Emotions

We have many emotions and each one satiates a particular need. Emotions are like nutrients such as vitamins, proteins, carbohydrates, minerals or fats that fulfil different types of emotional needs. There is no single relationship, which can take care of all our emotional needs. Hence, we have many types of relationships and each relationship is important in our life.

Every relationship is unique and fulfils us in a different way. The love of a mother can't be replaced by the love of a father or a spouse. You are always a child in the eyes of your parents and they are always willing to support you and give you their unconditional love.

The love from your children is unique. You are a hero in their eyes and you try your best to live up to that image. Even the love of daughters is different from the love of sons.

There is no relationship like friendship in this world. Friends fulfil many emotional needs. In fact, we share our joy and sorrows best with our friends.

We also share a unique relationship with our bosses because we learn from them and one day we would like to achieve their position. Our bosses train us to become better professionals.

The most gratifying relationship is often found between a husband and a wife. They can be a lover and a friend to each other. Often wives care for their husbands like a mother and husbands protect their wives like a father would. It is for this reason that when people fall in love, they feel elated and satisfied as they find almost all kinds of emotions present in their relationship with their beloved. When married couples have children, in their attempt to provide an ideal environment at home to their children, they become better and more responsible human beings.

If your relationship is supported on multiple feet, it is durable and stable. If you have only one in your life, your life is quite unstable and your emotions fragile. Once you have strong relations with people, you can share all types of emotions with them.

It is foolish to bare your heart before everyone. If you express your true emotions before everyone, you end up making a fool of yourself. You need intimate relations to share your deepest thoughts. An intimate person is one who understands you deeply and would not reveal your personal feelings to anyone else. Sharing your secrets with such a person only deepens the relationship further.

Let us say that you are having a very bad time with your boss and you wish to shout at him or even hit him. If you express your thoughts before your colleagues in office, they may tell your boss about it and antagonise your boss further. However, when you bare your emotions before a good friend or your spouse, you feel relieved because you have vented out your anger without it coming to the knowledge of your boss. Moreover, you may get their advice on how to tackle the situation and improve the relationship.

Sometimes we are angry with our close relatives like parents, children or spouse. It is not advisable to express your anger or wash your dirty linen in public. A famous poet Rahim has advised people,

Rahiman nij man ki vyatha, man hi rakhiyo goya
Suni ithilai hain log sab, baanti na laihen koya.

(It is wise to keep the pains in your heart,
than to speak of it in public.
People scoff at your misery,
but none may share your pain.)

If you keep your pain within your heart, you stand the risk of creating a deep wound in it. And so you must be able to share your deepest pain with people who are very close to you. The very act of sharing it with them reduces its severity. Sharing the pain in public can magnify it since numerous people will be talking about your pain. A famous Hindi song says, 'I am not pained by my troubles, but what pains me the most is that it is discussed by others.'

Intimate relationships are invaluable and they must be treasured like diamonds. John Lennon, iconic English singer and songwriter, had said, 'We've got this gift of love, but love is like a precious plant. You can't just accept it and leave it in the cupboard or just think it's going to get on by itself. You've got to keep watering it. You've got to really look after it and nurture it.'

Nurturing intimate relationships is one of the greatest sources of happiness and a key requirement for a happy life.

30

Conquer Your Boredom

The two enemies of human happiness are pain and boredom.
—Arthur Schopenhauer, German philosopher

We all know what boredom is because we all have experienced it at some point in time. Boredom may be defined as the state of being weary and restless through lack of interest. In simple words, when we don't like what we do, or we don't like to do anything, we are feeling bored.

Boredom is gripping the modern world rapidly because the technological developments over the last few centuries have increased the efficiencies and the productivity through machines, so much so that we have lots of free time at our disposal now. We don't know how to spend the surplus time in an interesting way.

There are millions of people in the modern world who have earned enough money to be able to live their lives comfortably without doing anything for a living.

However, most of them fail to live happily because they get bored if they do nothing. Many people don't work for the sake of money. They work to avoid boredom.

People would do anything to get rid of boredom. It has been linked to behaviour issues including bad driving, mindless snacking, binge drinking, risky sex and gambling. However, they can overcome their boredom only for a short period because as soon as the exciting activity is over, they start feeling bored again.

The Business of Boredom

The propensity of people to get bored with their lives has transformed the modern world. It feels as if the number of bored people has been increasing exponentially over the years. Our ancestors of hunter generation faced no boredom because they had to constantly chase wild animals for their survival. This was a daily task. In the agrarian society, people were busy round the year cultivating crops, protecting it from thieves and praying to God to give them the right amounts of sun and rain. However, the modern era has automated a large number of these processes and many people today have too much of time at their disposal. They don't know how to use this time. The wide prevalence of boredom in the modern world has given rise to numerous businesses.

- People got bored of eating home-made food, hence boomed the restaurant business.
- People got bored of the scenery around their home, hence boomed the tourism industry.

- People got bored of their routine life, hence boomed the entertainment world.
- People got bored with easy games, hence boomed the adventure games.

We can link the prosperity of many trades and industries around the world with boredom. There are hundreds of varieties of chocolates, biscuits, ice-creams available, and more being developed daily, because people get bored of the same flavour. Boredom is also responsible for flourishing of all sorts of entertainment including pornography.

Yet, people in the modern world are the most bored generation. They keep refreshing their Facebook, Instagram and Twitter pages to see if something interesting is happening. They would switch on their television sets every now and then with the hope to see some interesting content on it. If nothing works, they plan to dine out, go for a holiday or join a club to get rid of the boredom.

People seek new jobs, cars, music systems, televisions or house because they are tired of the existing ones. Their boredom gets alleviated when they are looking at the various options available in the market for these things and then trying to figure out the finance part of it—to buy it with down payment or EMI—and dreaming of the joy of having new things in their lives. However, their boredom is back again once they get used to their new acquisition. They start feeling miserable after their new possession becomes disinteresting.

You can't have boredom and happiness living under the same roof. If we are able to manage our boredom, we can easily manage our happiness. We can overcome our boredom by doing the following activities.

Develop an Interesting Routine

One of the best ways to get rid of boredom is to develop a routine that is interesting and has a variety of activities. You can include activities like walking, working-out, reading, writing, painting, watching TV and the like as part of your daily routine in addition to your regular work like going to office or household chores. When you don't have an interesting routine, you perform your tasks based on your moods or necessity. You get bored of the work soon. Once you are bored, you find it difficult to reboot your mind to an interesting level. When you have roped in a variety of work in your daily routine, all the tasks become interesting.

Follow Your Passion

When you have discovered your passion, you can always use it to change your mood. For example, I have a passion for writing. However, I am not always in the mood to write. Sometimes, I don't have any interesting thing to share. Nonetheless, I force myself to write anyway in the fixed hour of the day. And most of the times, once I get down to writing, I start enjoying it as the creative thoughts start flowing in my mind. I get deeply involved and the boredom evaporates. If you have a passion, you can use it anytime to overcome your monotony by just getting into the grove.

Set Ambitious Goals

The problem with all the external means of stimulation to overcome boredom is that they are for a short duration. A movie gets over in about two hours, a football match lasts only for ninety minutes and most TV shows are for less than an hour. You can't enjoy the best foods and drinks for long as their excess can lead to health problems. Just like you get a hangover after consuming alcohol, you get a hangover after all forms of external stimulants. Your ability to enjoy the same activities diminishes every time and you need higher doses of stimulations to experience the same level of joy.

However, if you have a long-term goal in your life, all your activities become a part of that goal. You can keep yourself engaged for several hours and even days when you are reading an interesting book. When you are writing your new book, you can be busy for a year. When you want to transform the society, help the needy, educate the poor children, your goal can keep you engaged fruitfully for life.

The greater is your goal, the higher is your energy level for achieving the goal and the less time you have to get bored.

Be Creative

You can view boredom not as a source of pain, but a luxury available to only a selected few. Most people are so busy in their routine jobs that they have no time for their friends, family and even for themselves. When you are getting bored, it means that you have time for yourself. When you are with yourself, you can listen to your soul and become creative.

Most of us are so used to living amidst the noise of modern life that we have forgotten the value of silence. Imagine that you switch off all the fans and ACs at your home. You can now hear the slightest sound of the horn from a vehicle plying on the road, or a conversation between people or the crying of a child in your neighbourhood. When it is night and the silence is deep, you can hear the ticking of your clock. When the silence is even deeper, you can even hear the vibrations of the universe and the beating of your own heart.

You get in touch with the world and yourself at the deepest level when you are surrounded by silence. The extreme of boredom thus prompts you to become creative.

When human beings got bored, they created new cities, discovered the laws of the world, made beautiful paintings, wrote books and developed philosophies.

If we can suffer boredom with peace and conquer it with patience, we can discover our creative selves. Robert M Pirsig, author of *Zen and the Art of Motorcycle Maintenance* said this beautifully, 'Boredom always precedes a period of great creativity.'

Conquer Boredom

If you wish to be happy for life, you have to conquer boredom. Instead of using any artificial external stimulants such as movies, drinks, drugs or dining-out to avoid boredom, you can use boredom to be creative and engage in activities such as writing a book, doing a good research, innovating a product or creating a new piece of music. If you set a long-term goal for making the world a better place, you can push away boredom and not face unhappiness in your life.

31

Make Your Own Path

If you're walking down the right path and you're willing to keep walking, eventually you'll make progress.

—Barack Obama, former President of USA

If you ask people what they want in life, most of them would give you some vague answers like:

- I want to be happy
- I want to be rich
- I want to be powerful enough to change the world
- I want to take care of my family
- I want to serve my country
- I want to spread love in the world
- I want to remove hatred
- I want peace

Most people don't really know what they want and why they want something. Hence, everything seems desirable.

As they can never achieve everything, they remain unhappy throughout their lives.

People often want perfection for themselves and their worlds. They want a world free from all troubles, problems and challenges. Since the world can't be perfect, these people are seldom happy.

People keep chasing different things in life and keep getting pushed by different people and situations. They move in 'Brownian motion' in random directions travelling all the time but reaching nowhere.

When we depend on the outside world for our happiness, there are billions of causes that can take away our joy. We need to find an anchor which can tie us to our happiness like a ship is tied to the shoreline. We need to board this big ship to achieve stability and protect ourselves from the uncertain waves of life.

Set Your Goal

In order to avoid losing our focus with every small incident of joy or sorrow, we require something steadier to bank upon. We need to accomplish a goal and have to choose a path to travel. James Allen, the famous British philosophical writer, said in his book *As a Man Thinketh*:

> They who have no central purpose in their life fall an easy prey to petty worries, fears, troubles and self-pitying, all of which are indications of weakness, which lead, just as surely as deliberately planned sins (though by a different route), to failure, unhappiness and loss, for weakness cannot persist in a power evolving universe.

We need to have goals which can be accomplished in reasonable time. Goals could be short-term, medium-term and long-term.

The short-term goals can be compared with seasonal crops that get ready within a few months. There are several actions that can give result in a short duration. For example, if you have to control your weight, you must immediately start controlling your diet and doing your workouts or yoga practices. You will start seeing the effect of your actions within a month or so. You can develop the habit of reading, or spending more time with your family and friends and you can see the benefits very soon.

Short-term goals can make your life better but it is not easy to pursue them since they need change of habits. The good news is that you can change your habits if you push yourself against your will repeatedly. Your actions will gradually transform your thoughts and you will develop new habits. What looks difficult and painful in the beginning, due to a change of habit, will become easy and joyful once the new habits are formed.

Long-term goals are like planting a tree that will bear fruits only after a few years. These trees take a long time to grow but they provide lasting benefits. Unlike the seasonal crop that gives you benefits only once, the trees keep bearing fruits year after year without much effort. However, you have to constantly work for a couple of years even when no fruit is in sight. You must have faith and the motivation to be able to put in continuous effort for a long time.

In order to develop long-term goals, you need to sow good thoughts immediately and let your soul be transformed by the growth of your thoughts as you start putting them into practice. James Allen said, 'Every thought-seed sown or allowed to fall into the mind, and to take root there, produces its own, blossoming sooner or later into act, and bearing its own fruitage of opportunity and circumstance. Good thoughts bear good fruit, bad thoughts bad fruit.'

The long-term investments include:

- Sowing good thoughts in the mind.
- Taking care of your family, parents and children.
- Being faithful to your spouse.
- Developing the habit of keeping your word and walking your talk.
- Selflessly helping others.

When you read good books, interact with good people, you are sowing the seeds of good thoughts in your mind. You also need to water them daily till they take deep roots in your mind. You have to provide them with plenty of sunshine, air and nutrients regularly. When their roots go deep, they can draw all nutrition and water on their own and no effort or very little effort will be required from your end.

If you fail to sow good thoughts in your mind, the weeds of evil thoughts will take root there and eventually they will take up all the space and not let good thoughts flourish.

All goals take time to be accomplished. Think a hundred times before setting up your goals. However, once you decide, don't change the goal in a hurry. Don't abandon goals after you have travelled a long distance on them. We waste lot of time and energy in pursuing goals that are either not suitable for us, or we are not suitable for them. Only when our thoughts are matured, our vision is clear, can we follow long-term goals.

Find Meaning of Your Life

Your goals can't be accomplished unless they are in harmony with you and with the world. The world is not interested in fulfilling your desires. It is interested in fulfilling its own desires. When I am referring to the world, I mean every living being in it; be it human beings or animals. Even if we are bound to die one day, yet we are part of the flame that is going to pass unto the eternity from one generation to another.

We don't only pass on our genes to our children; we pass on our thoughts too. We are playing a unique role in this world because the world would be incomplete without us. Once we understand that we are irreplaceable for our parents, beloved, spouse, children, friends and even our society, we can, instead of carrying on merely with our lives find a deeper purpose for being in this world. Viktor E Frankl, Austrian neurologist and psychiatrist said,

> It did not really matter what we expected from life, but rather what life expected from us. We needed to stop asking

> about the meaning of life, and instead to think of ourselves as those who were being questioned by life—daily and hourly. Our answer must consist, not in talk and meditation, but in right action and in right conduct. Life ultimately means taking the responsibility to find the right answer to its problems and to fulfil the tasks which it constantly sets for each individual.

While setting your goal keeps you focused, search for meaning keeps the world in focus. You can't avoid your responsibilities for personal convenience and set to lead a life that is full of indifference to the world. Let us remember that we would not have survived even for a few days but for the love and care of our parents. We would have learned nothing much more than what an ape knows, unless we had been taught by our teachers. We have been nourished by the unconditional love of our parents, elders, siblings, teachers and others. Hence, to discard all our responsibility and run away from life would be an act of cowardice and ungratefulness.

Setting your goal and finding a meaning of your life are not two different things as they are interdependent.

- Can a businessman become rich if he does not know what the consumer wants?
- Can an author become successful unless he knows what readers want?

There are always two sides of every coin; one that is inside (you) and the other that is outside (world). When you know the meaning of your life, you can also discover the goal of your life. Nietzsche, the famous German philosopher, has rightly said, 'He who has a "Why" to live for can bear almost any "How".'

Define Your Principles

You must have certain principles in life to ensure that you follow the right path and do not deviate from it at the time of difficulties. Principles are not meant so much for the easy times, as for the difficult times, when you are tempted to follow the easy path to avoid the pressing problem.

Often you can save yourself from a problem by simply telling a lie. A lie, however, has no impact if the person is known to be a liar. Only a person with reputation of honesty is benefited from a lie since people believe his words to be true based on his past track record. However, once the lie is detected, the person loses all prospective benefits that lying may have brought in the future.

It is important for us to define our principles which are in harmony with our goals and meaning of life. We must bring ourselves under the protection of our principles in order to bring discipline to our life. We must honour our principles with courage and conviction.

Develop Your Philosophy of Life

It is important to understand our limitations as a mortal human being while choosing our goals in life. Reinhold Niebuhr, an American theologian, ethicist and public intellectual said, 'God, grant me the serenity to accept the things I cannot change, the courage to change the things I can, and the wisdom to know the difference.'

We often see injustice and inequality all around. There are people who live like kings and there are those who are in a state worse than animals. When we are on the receiving end of injustice, we fight against it. Even when we are not affected, we may still want to help the people who are victims. However, when we try to help everyone, we make our own lives miserable. James Allen rightly warned, 'A strong man cannot help a weaker unless that weaker is willing to be helped, and even then the weak man must become strong of himself; he must, by his own efforts, develop the strength which he admires in another. None but himself can alter his condition.'

It needs considerable wisdom to understand your ability to handle the numerous problems of the world. It is foolish to take the responsibility of everything wrong out there and then feel crushed under its burden.

Instead of expecting an ideal world, we must learn to live in the real world. Instead of making our life miserable for the sake of others, we must learn to make our own lives joyful. We can give only what we have. If we are unhappy, we can't make others happy. When we have no love in our heart, we can't love anyone. You can't gift wealth to anyone unless you earn it yourself.

We must, therefore, develop a philosophy of life which balances our needs with the needs of the world, our joys with the joys of the world and our selflessness with the selfishness of the world. You can never meet the expectations of people. People will anyway criticise you if you are wealthy, powerful or even happy. Your philosophy must be balanced to take care of your external and internal worlds.

Your philosophy must be moral and according to your principles and deepest values. It must guide your actions for a more fulfilled life. For example, non-violence was the philosophy of Gandhi and he lived by it. You may agree or disagree with his philosophy but his philosophy guided him throughout his life. Every great person followed his own philosophy to lead his life. These philosophies are often named after the persons who lived by them. So you have Gandhism, Buddhism, Nazism, Marxism as some of the philosophies that shaped the world. You must develop your own philosophy that is in tune with the time and also with your own nature to shape your life.

References and Bibliography

1: Happiness is a Choice

1. Carver, Courtney. 'The Story of the Mexican Fisherman', https://bemorewithless.com/the-story-of-the-mexican-fisherman

2: Happiness is a Stream of Experiences

1. Parthasarathy, A. *The Holocaust of Attachment: Vedanta World,* (2014).

3: Happiness is Subjective

1. Hanh, Thich Nhat. 'Zen Buddhist Questions and Answers: Space and Freedom', http://www.katinkahesselink.net/tibet/thich-freedom.html

5: The Source for Joy and Sorrow are the Same

1. Funny Jokes: http://funnydb.net/joke/it-seems-that-reagan-and-gorbachev-arranged-a-competition-to-determ-60216
2. Hercules and Plutus, 'Aesop's Fable', https://www.wattpad.com/14476-aesop%27s-fables-a-new-translation/page/51
3. Klien, Christopher. 'Mussolini's Final Hours, 70 Years Ago', http://www.history.com/news/mussolinis-final-hours-70-years-ago
4. McGowan, Norman. 'My Years with CHURCHILL', https://archive.org/stream/myyearswithchurc006753mbp/myyearswithchurc006753mbp_djvu.txt

5. Gibran, Kahlil. *The Prophet* (On Joy and Sorrow), http://www.katsandogz.com/onjoy.html

6: Comparison is Injurious to Happiness

1. *Isha Upanishad*, http://www.swamij.com/upanishad-isha-purna.htm

7: Lying Leads to Unhappiness

1. Cathecart, Thomas and Klein, Denial. 'Plato and a Platypus Walk into a Bar: Understanding Philosophy Through Jokes', Penguin Books, USA (2008).
2. Newspaper interview (1902), when asked, Halle, Kay, Irrepressible Churchill. Cleveland: World, 1966, cited in *Churchill by Himself* (2008), Langworth (ed.), Public Affairs, p. 489, ISBN 1586486381.

9: Earn Honestly, Spend Wisely

1. Joshi, Manik (2014-01-25). Best Jokes: I Have Ever Heard—888 Jokes (Kindle Locations 1796-1799). Kindle Edition.

11: Be the Master of Law

1. Sufism/Nasrudin, https://en.wikibooks.org/wiki/Sufism/Nasrudin

13: Manage Your Love

1. Allison, Joy. *Which Loved Best*, http://www.english-for-students.com/Which-Loved-Best.html

17: Anger Destroys Happiness

1. Mills, Harry. 'Physiology Of Anger', (2005) https://www.mentalhelp.net/articles/physiology-of-anger
2. Gilliss, Trent T. 'The Little Monk and the Samurai: A Zen Parable', https://onbeing.org/blog/trent-gilliss-the-little-monk-and-the-samurai-a-zen-parable/
3. Temper, Zen Koans, http://www.ashidakim.com/zenkoans/75temper.html

21: Invest in Suffering

1. Gilbert, Daniel. *Stumbling on Happiness*, Vintage Publication.

23: Forgive and Forget

1. Singh, Awdhesh. *Timeless Jokes—Ageless Wisdom*, The Aatmic Science Foundation, (2014).

24: Develop the Habit of Giving

1. Joshi, Manik (2014-01-25). Best Jokes: I Have Ever Heard—888 Jokes (Kindle Locations 1796-1799). Kindle Edition.

25: Count Your Blessings

1. Gandhi, MK. An Autobiography or The Story of My Experiments, https://biblio.wiki/wiki/An_Autobiography_or_The_Story_of_my_Experiments_with_Truth

26. Restrict Your Options

1. Loss Aversion http://ui-patterns.com/patterns/Loss-aversion
2. Gilbert, Dan. 'TED Talk: The Surprising Science of Happiness' https://www.ted.com/talks/dan_gilbert_asks_why_are_we_happy#t-124636
3. Synthetic Happiness, Sources of Light, http://sourcesofinsight.com/synthetic-happiness/

28. Nurture Your Potentialities

1. Carrel, Alexis. 'Man, The Unknown', (1935).
2. 'Cristiano Ronaldo Dresses Up as a Homeless Man and Pranks Madrid with his Football Skills', *The Telegraph*, https://www.telegraph.co.uk/sport/football/players/cristiano-ronaldo/11782192/Cristiano-Ronaldo-dresses-up-as-a-homeless-man-and-pranks-Madrid-with-football-skills.html
3. Singh, Awdhesh. *Timeless Jokes—Ageless Wisdom*, The Aatmic Science Foundation, (2014).

30. Conquer Your Boredom

1. Schubert. 'Boredom as an Antagonist of Creativity', *Journal of Creative Behavior*, December 1977.
2. Mann and Cadman. 'Does Being Bored Make Us More Creative?', *Creativity Research Journal*, May 2014.
3. Stewart, Jude. 'Boredom Is Good for You 'The Surprising Benefits of Stultification', 2017, https://www.theatlantic.com/magazine/archive/2017/06/make-time-for-boredom/524514/